Anton's
Dance Class

Anton's Dance Class

with photography by Gregory King

Anton Du Beke

with a foreword by Len Goodman

Kyle Cathie Limited

To my brother Stephen, my sister Veronica and mostly my Mum - without her what would I be?

First published in Great Britain in 2007 by
Kyle Cathie Limited
122 Arlington Road, London NW1 7HP
www.kylecathie.com

10 9 8 7 6 5 4 3 2

ISBN 978 1 85626 731 1

Designer: Geoff Hayes
Photography: Gregory King
Artwork: David Downton
Make up: Jo Jenkins and Anna Winterburn
Picture research: Kellee Hubbert

Colour reproduction by Scanhouse, Malaysia
Printed and bound in Great Britain by Butler and Tanner

I would like to thank all the teachers who've given me lessons: amongst many, Beryl and Velda Holton, Bill and Sylvia Mitchell, Bob and Barbara Grover, Michael and Lorna Stylianos, Richard and Janet Gleave, Anne Gleave, Michael and Vicky Barr, Anthony Hurley, Marcus and Karen Hilton, and John Del-roy.

Caroline Feraday and Sophie Allen helped me get the words onto the page. Louise keeps me out of trouble and tries to get me there on time; without her I'd be nothing. Thanks too to Greg for his fabulous pictures, David for depicting us in art. Geoff for his designs. Flavia for her body and Erin – I am only half a man without Erin. Len – thanks for the Foreword.

Thanks to Tony Brackley for the suits, Supadance for the shoes, DSI for the frocks – you're good to Erin and me. And to my friends Stuart Rach and of course, Jeff.

Contents

Foreword

I have known Anton almost all of his dancing life. I remember first seeing him dance at the Rivoli Ballroom when he was little more than a beginner. It was clear then that Anton had the talent and potential to become a Champion. Talent, however, is not the only element of becoming a great dancer – tenacity and the will to win are also paramount if you are going to reach your goal.

So, when asked by Anton to read through his new book on Ballroom and Latin Dancing, of course I said I would be delighted but in fact it filled me with dread; not only for myself but for all those poor suckers trying to grasp the basic steps from all the technical jargon, intricate step patterns and complex timings. How wrong I was – this book is a joy. At last a chance to learn the basic moves in a clear, uncluttered way and not over technical but as Alex Moore (a famous dance teacher and inventor of the Whisk move in the Waltz) once said, 'A beginner should only learn the steps before trying to master the technique'.

Each dance has a potted history of its roots (it's worth reading just for this). The foot positions, alignments and turns are explained clearly.

This is a most excellent book for the beginner, who is setting out on the road to Ballroom and Latin dancing success. It is a great appetiser, giving the reader a taste of the excitement and glamour of dancing.

Good reading and happy dancing!

Len Goodman

Introduction

Most fourteen year old boys play football and aspire to playing professionally when they're older. I was no different. Until a chance glance at my sister's dance class revealed that it was packed full of girls! Like many dance classes – especially before the phenomenon that is *Strictly Come Dancing* – the girls way outnumbered the boys and I was roped into helping out with a dance number after simply going to meet her for the walk home.

It was the *Sliding Doors* moment that inspired my career, and hopefully one such moment will inspire you to take to the dance floor. This book is my opportunity to share with you my love of dancing, and dancing with a partner, and I hope it's something which you'll stick with for at least as long as I have. After all, that chance opportunity was five years ago now...

I know that I joke about starting dancing for the girls in the class, but there is something very special about dancing with a partner. One of my own personal favourite things about dancing is that feeling of harmony and unison on the dance floor. And it's been an incredible experience and great privilege to be teamed up with Lesley Garrett, Esther Rantzen, Patsy Palmer and Jan Ravens in the past four series of hit BBC series *Strictly Come Dancing*; all experts at what they do, but virgins on the dance floor. It was a real gamble as to whether this sequined celebrity fest would capture the public's imagination. Of course, I'm pleased to say it did and with record audience figures for the previous four series we're now looking forward to a fifth series later this year.

In this book I'll showcase the ten Ballroom and Latin American dances and, unlike the learn-to-dance books which just show you a series of steps, I really want to give you the opportunity to discover for yourself how it feels to dance.

If you've never danced before then this is the perfect opportunity to begin – in the comfort of your own front room! Then imagine the

look on your friend's faces when you next take to the dance floor! Or if you have some experience of dancing, I'm sure you'll find the exercises and suggestions here useful for taking your dancing to another level. There really is something for everyone from complete beginner to experienced dancer. All the exercises and suggestions featured here are ones that I do with my *Strictly Come Dancing* celebrity partners, who have never danced before but they are also the ones that I regularly practice with Erin Boag, my professional dance partner.

I hope you find a good partner too. Erin and I have been dancing together for quite some time now and together we've travelled the world. The relationship you have with your dance partner is truly unique and I hope this book will be the start of a wonderful partnership for you too.

And you'll find that dancing is not only incredibly rewarding when you get to show off on the dance floor, but also for your waist line. There's no better way to stay fit and healthy without feeling like you've exercised at all!

I look forward to being part of this fun, healthy and rewarding experience with you.

Welcome to my dance class. Now this book is going to be a gentle introduction to Ballroom and Latin American dancing where we are going to have some fun without getting too bogged down in the technical jargon, but also give ourselves the sense of how it feels to dance because that great feeling of exhilaration that comes with moving across the floor in total harmony with your partner and spinning, turning, twirling, jiving is the most important thing. If you want high-level technique, go and have a lesson at a dance studio but, if you want to get a sense of how to dance and feel fabulous with it, read on. Hopefully this book will give you the confidence to join a local dance class and take your dancing to the next level. Dancing is a wonderful way of socialising, keeping fit and enjoying yourself.

After all, we're now going into our fifth series of BBC's *Strictly Come Dancing* and I can already begin to feel the excitement and anticipation; it has been such a pleasure to find so many dance classes full as the result of the enthusiasm for Ballroom and Latin American dancing that has been sparked by the series. Those 13 million fans can't all be wrong! Watch the great movies – *Top Hat, Singing in the Rain, An American in Paris* – anything with Fred Astaire, Ginger Rogers or Cyd Charisse; Gene Kelly and Donald O'Connor are other greats.

Now, good dancing requires a few basic fundamentals. Here are the bits to think about time and again when you're getting in the mood to dance.

Posture

Posture is vitally important because the better the posture, the better the dancing; it is so much easier to dance with good posture. Bad posture leads to many problems – you'll be kicking each other half to death and won't be speaking by the end of the night. Good posture helps balance, the leading, the following and the transferring of weight – the overall movement. So, how do we stand? When you lift your arms into dance position make sure you don't lift your shoulders too. Boys first, stand with your feet together and standing tall, make sure your head, shoulders, chest and hips are lined up over each other over the centre of the foot and with your ribcage lifted and your arms hanging down by your side. Ladies, do the same thing. At this point, ladies, you might feel like you're sticking your chest out, but you're not, you're just standing correctly. There's something we call sunken chest syndrome; pick up your ribcage because it releases your hips and don't try to 'hide' your chest. Posture for the ladies is not to be confused with poise – we will come to that in a minute. And when you're dancing around the floor try and maintain your perfect posture. A quick word of advice for the boys: ladies like a man who stands tall, which makes him look elegant and refined, even if he's not in real life. You get a much better feel for the dance with good posture. New dancers particularly feel uncomfortable by the invasion of their space, more so with Latin American, but this can be helped by good posture too.

Poise

The poise of the body will add to the look and the balance of your dancing. For the ladies, in Ballroom, the poise is a slight curve to your left, with your head turned very slightly so that you can look over your wrist to the left but with your head continuing the line of your spine. For the boys, the body should be leaning slightly forward. It's also important for boys and girls not to allow the weight of the body to be rocked onto the heels – always feel like you are on the middle to the front of your foot. In Latin American dancing, the body should be poised very slightly forwards for both boy and girl.

Sway

This is simply an inclination of the body to the left or to the right, used mainly to balance yourself, but it can be used for effect and to add a bit of drama in a Ballroom dance, or in a Latin such as the Paso Doble, a nice look to a line or a position, generally a bit of quality – and it gives you a great feeling when you do a sway in harmony. The dynamic of balance is the better the dancer the better the sway they can do and sway always involves the whole body and legs, never being done just from the waist.

Footwork

This is just a description of the heel or stepping onto the ball of your foot or your toes in contact with the floor during individual steps – whether you're stepping onto an individual part of the foot. There are four parts of the foot used in great Ballroom and Latin dancing – toe, ball of the foot, flat foot (whole of it) and the heel. Never try to put your weight onto the outside edge of the foot until you're a professional dancer. It's good to get the right footwear – dancing shoes – some are a bit pretty and not very useful, some have good soles, made of a soft suede finish – of course it's easier to use your feet with better shoes and it makes you a better dancer. Start with something that stays on your feet – sounds obvious but you should see what they wear to my classes. Sling backs are a no! Court shoes without too high a heel are good and they add to the stability of your dance.

Rise and Fall

This interprets musicality and goes a little bit hand-in-glove with footwork, and describes elevation created by the straightening of the legs; when I rise onto my toes, I start to straighten my

leg and stretch my body. Every Ballroom dance apart from Tango has the need for rise and fall – and I have described it in some detail in the exercise for the Waltz on pages 62–63.

Weight

It is true to say that when travelling forwards the weight of the body should be forwards, when travelling sideways, the weight of the body should be forwards, when travelling backwards, the weight of the body should be… forwards. I think you could say there is a pattern forming.

We are going to discuss the transferring of weight a lot in this book because when people learn to dance they learn to fully transfer weight properly. The weight of the body should fully transfer from one foot to the other; at no time should the weight be split between the two feet. The elegance of dancing comes from having the weight on only one foot at a time and truly transferring the whole body weight with each step.

Balance

When you move forwards or backwards, good balance makes for elegance and ease of movement; it is probably the most important element of making you a good dancer. It means that the carriage of your weight is in the right place. It means that your body can move freely and your legs can swing freely from the hips. Think about it as you learn and relax along the way.

The Hold

How do you hold? Boys, we're getting to the good bit now, this is where you're allowed to touch your partner but you've got to do it nicely, otherwise the ladies will talk about you in the powder room. In the Ballroom hold, stand with the feet slightly apart, boys start off by raising the left arm so that the hand is slightly above the level of the shoulder, with the elbow slightly bent. The right hand should be placed just on or below the lady's left shoulder blade with the man's right elbow picked up to match the height of his left elbow, without of course, lifting the shoulders. It makes for a much better line and makes you look like you know what you're doing, which helps. Now ladies, you raise your right arm up, placing your right hand in the man's left hand, palm to palm, slightly bending your right elbow. Then you place your left hand on the man's upper right arm, below his shoulder. Stand in front of your partner in a slightly offset position with your right fronts facing each other (i.e. slightly to the right side of the man). The normal hold in Latin American dancing is the exactly the same hold but you stand about a foot apart (rather than the bodies touching).

Hands and Arms and Feet

Now I know this is something that is discussed a lot on BBC's *Strictly*. It seems Arlene Philips has got a particular fascination with hands and arms. When you are not holding your partner, use your hands and arms in such a way you don't look like an octopus falling out of a tree. Hold them out, extended all the way to the fingertips. The arms don't finish at the wrist, they finish at the fingertips, which completes the line. There has to be a softness but without them being floppy, so with tone. Now if you do this, I'm sure that if you ever get a chance to dance in front of Arlene, she will be overwhelmed with the arms; it's just the other stuff she might have a problem with.

Finish off the line of your body through your feet – particularly important in Latin. In Ballroom, go

away and practise your walk – we're not flipper feet, we're dancing gods!

The Walk

The perfect walk is what we are trying to achieve. Now I appreciate that when you walk down the high street you won't walk like this (well I do, but what else would you expect?) so let's be realistic and start with the getting to the bus walk and we can work up to the Anton Walk. But if you get this walk perfected, think how fabulously you will be able to dance.

Through each of the dances I've incorporated an exercise. Some of the exercises are basic figures that I believe develop the whole feeling of the dance and others are just the walk, which we've highlighted in greater detail below. Whatever they are, they are good exercise too. The great thing about the walk is that it incorporates all the points that we need to keep thinking about – posture, transference of weight and timing are the key elements – and if you can perfect these basics then you will get the feeling of being a dancer. One of the great joys of dancing is to feel the dancing. And you don't have to be a great dancer to feel great dancing.

The walk is a major part of Ballroom dancing and begins with the feet closed and the weight equally balanced, with the knees slightly flexed. The body starts to move first, the man stepping forward with the ball of the moving foot skimming the floor, going onto the heel at the same time the heel of the supporting foot releases. The weight is now central on both feet and I call this the Johnny Walker (man on the bottle of Whisky) moment – on the heel of the front foot and the ball of the back foot, passing through as the front foot goes flat taking the weight of the body, the back foot is pulled up from the toe, then ball of foot, going flat as it passes the standing foot. Ladies, remember that the man is leading and in control, and you are moving as one.

Now the backward walk starts again with the feet together, knees slightly flexed and weight equally apportioned. The leg swinging backwards from the hip extends to the toe, then moves onto the ball, with the weight of the body remaining on the front foot. As you start to transfer the weight, the weight rolls from the toe of the back foot onto the ball, and at the same time releases the toe and the ball of the front foot; at this stage the knee of the front leg will be straight and the back knee somewhat flexed. The weight is now passing through central position with the weight on both the heel of the front foot and the ball of the back foot. Continuing, the heel of the front foot is lightly drawn towards the back foot skimming across the floor, whilst the heel of the back foot only lowers when the front foot (which is now flat) passes underneath you.

Alignment and Direction

This is about the feet and which way they are travelling and the alignment also relates to the way you are facing in the room at the end of the step. The diagram shows you the basics; it can get more complicated for experienced dancers but this will get you off the starting blocks and covers the dance steps in this book.

1: Facing diagonally to centre
2: Facing line of dnace
3: Facing diagonally to wall
4: Facing centre
5: Facing wall

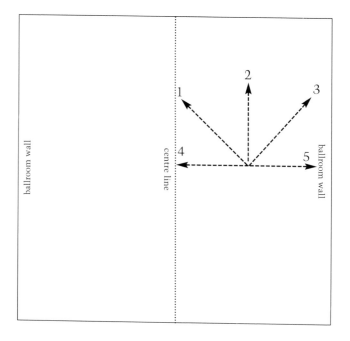

Leading and Following

I was once told that a good man follows what he leads, so boys, not only do you have to lead but you have to follow as well. There's a correct time to lead and an incorrect time to lead. The correct time is when you're taking a step: so, take a step and go from there. Once contact between partners is made, leading is through moving the hand to direct her to move as you will. Leading is a whole body experience – you can't just use one bit of your body – your leg or your hips, you've got to use everything. So, as you're taking a step and you want to turn to the right, for example, you take a step forward with your right foot and you must turn your whole body as well, indicating to the lady that you want to turn that way. I know it sounds like a simple thing but unless you turn everything you will find the message won't get across and you'll kick her, you'll run into her, she won't turn the correct way, simply because you are not leading properly. Now, ladies, what you have to do is pay attention to the lead, not anticipate or guess too much because he might change his mind.

Music

You may hear different things about music in Ballroom dancing. It is strict tempo because the speed of the music remains consistent throughout the dance. There is also time signature – how many beats and bars there are in a piece of music, for example in the Waltz it is 3/4 time, that's to say there are 3 beats in each bar of music. The Foxtrot and Quickstep are in 4/4 time, so there are 4 beats in each bar of music but, although they both have 4 beats in a bar, you cannot use the same piece of music because the tempos are different, with the Quickstep being almost double the speed. And the same goes for the Latin dances. The Cha Cha Cha and the Rumba are both in 4/4 time but the Rumba is much slower in tempo. Ballroom begins on the first beat in the bar, whereas, in the true spirit of Latin dances, it begins on the second beat of the bar.

Tempo

At its simplest, tempo is the speed at which the music is played or the number of bars per minute. The Viennese Waltz has around 52 bars to the minute whereas the Waltz has only 32 bars to the minute. Now, some bands play faster than others and, as a rule of thumb, for those that play faster than average, you should shorten the steps proportionately and, for those playing slower, then you should lengthen the steps appropriately.

Rhythm

The rhythm of the music refers to the recurring and accentuated beats and the length of the individual musical notes. It can also refer to

whether you're dancing in time with the music or not, as the case may be! It's what gives dance life, colour and soul for me.

Ballroom and Latin American

The biggest difference with Ballroom and Latin dancing is the proximity, which seems bizarre because in Latin you are further apart. But the similarities are many – you still need to have good posture, great balance, transfer your weight, be in good time, lead your partner well, follow well – the major difference is the hold. Sometimes you let go of each other altogether.

There is usually more of a narrative in the Latin dances and Rumba is the dance of love; Ballroom is more about motion and the movement of the dance than the suggestion of the choreography. There is a formality to the Ballroom dances, with the style of the dress and the fact that you don't actually look at each other. In Ballroom, there is a sense of one body, moving together in harmony, with the man moving for the lady. The movement, pattern and flow of the steps gives it the musicality of beauty. In Latin, the bodies move together but not in such harmonious unity, and there's more of a story. There is more interaction between boy and girl in the Latin dances – you get to look at each other.

How to Construct Dances

The construction of dances is like learning a language – the more words you learn, the better your vocabulary is, and dancing is exactly the same – the more steps you master the better and more developed the dance routine will be. You have to develop your vocabulary i.e. the steps, and then away you go from there. You are limited by the foot you have available as to what you can do.

So, in Ballroom, if you have your right foot available you will be turning invariably to the right, and if you have your left foot available you will be turning invariably to the left; sounds obvious, I know, but there will not be a time when you step forwards on your right foot and turn to the left. And the same applies for the Latin.

Once you've learnt the steps, then start to learn on which foot you will finish each of the steps; then you can start putting the dance steps together and building your sentences. For example, in the Foxtrot or the Waltz, you do a natural turn to the right which is 6 steps and boys, you start with the right foot, so that at the end of the 6 steps, the right foot will be available. To make a left foot available, you will then add a change step. Then perhaps you might go into a reverse turn, another 6 steps, and add a change step before going into a natural turn. Or you could do a whisk, with the left foot available, and from a whisk do a chassé followed by a natural turn.

The creation of a dance depends on 3 things: Firstly, if you know your partner and how experienced each of you is. Secondly, the floor plan, who else is moving about on it and what space is available. Thirdly, knowledge of which step finishes on which foot and which foot you will have available to lead off on.

For each of the dances I have given you a routine of steps to get you going. You'll find these on the first step of each of the dances.

Here are a couple of terms that will appear throughout the book that I think you should definitely get to grips with right at the beginning.

Promenade Position

The boy's right side and lady's left side are in contact at the ribcage level with the opposite sides of the body turned out to form a V. In Latin, it's exactly the same apart from the fact that the bodies are not in contact, just joined by the hands, but only facing each other with the opposite sides still turned out to form a V.

In Line

To step between your partner's feet, for the man and the lady.

Outside Partner

To step to the side of your partner's feet, not in line.

I have always had a philosophy in dancing that the best way to improve quickly is not to dance with the same dancer all the time, so the best thing to do is ask other people to dance. So chaps, when you get the opportunity, take it. She will say yes, she's there to dance and she'll be thrilled, especially if you listen to what I tell you in the book. If you have good posture and good timing you will be the Anton of the Ballroom – a badge you should wear with pride. And remember ladies, you are not allowed to refuse: it's just not the Ballroom way.

Line of Dance

Once you've got dancing, you've taken hold, you've started to walk, you've got some music, you now need to know where to go, you need some direction – what we call the line of dance. The line of dance is very important because it's the direction in which we move around the floor. Some dances are slightly more stationary – the Rumba, the Jive, the Cha Cha Cha – but in the progressive dances like the Samba, the Paso Doble and all the Ballroom dances you need to move anti-clockwise around the floor, because you never move around the floor against the line of dance – it would be like going up a one-way street the wrong way. The key is to be flexible too – if you see a couple who are going to be in your way, boys, take the lead and dance a step that will get you out of trouble – I say collisions are only for the weak and not for me! Ladies, if you see a clash coming up, signal somehow to your partner!

Judging Dance

With an expert eye you can weigh up so much at a glance; most things break down because of technique – miscommunication between partners, poor alignment, bad posture…. Style, musicality, movement, major things are affected by a number of circumstances – are you together, out of time (might as well be shot with a big gun). You get more of a surprise when you come off thinking 'What a nightmare!' and then get good marks – you dodged a bullet there. In the early stages of a competition judging is done by a series of ticks but no marks and you either get through to the finals or you don't, whereas in the finals it's done by points and places are awarded for the first six.

Taking Dancing Further

Once you've got the bug, join a local dance studio; I've listed a few websites at the end of the book to help you on your way. Watch old movies, dance show reels, go to the dance demonstrations all over the country – who knows, you might even find me there! My heroes are the people who inspire me. Fred Astaire and Gene Kelly for all of us. Watch them now and they still look brilliant. Even now I go, 'This was 70 years ago, this is the nuts, utterly wonderful.'. Nureyev, Baryshinkov –

what great spinners. Sammy Davis Junior you can watch forever. Bruce Forsyth – a complete hero of mine, and to get to work with him is just a joy. Marcus Hilton, one of my teachers, makes me go – oh my god, he's so brilliant. People get blown away by clever footwork and choreography, but it is the body movement that makes dancing. I've danced with world champions from the 1970s onwards, greats such as Janet Gleave, Vicky Barr, Karen Hilton, Anne Gleave. It's also been great dancing with girls not from my world, ballerinas such as Lauren Cuthbertson; dancing with Bonny Langford too is a great experience.

What I hope that you will get from working with my book and watching the DVD is that great feeling of dance, of the exhilaration, the excitement, the fabulous feeling of everything important in the dance coming together.

The Foxtrot

Let's start with a hard one. If you can do the Foxtrot then the rest of the dances will feel so easy! Yes, this is the most difficult, but it's also my personal favourite. For me, it's THE dance.

I'll assume for a moment that you've got perfect posture. If you haven't, then do read the posture notes (see page 10). So for starters, make sure you're standing correctly and no doubt you'll be looking wonderful.

Secondly, can you walk in a straight line? If so, then you can dance the Foxtrot. Admittedly, I've described this dance as the most difficult, but it's also based on a walking action!

By the end of this chapter, you will have an insight and, I hope, a sense of how it feels to dance the Foxtrot. Obviously I need to explain to you the actual steps, and I will do, but you can read that in any book! I want you to get emotionally and physically connected with this dance and feel at least a little of what I feel, when I dance the Foxtrot.

So, you're standing up. You've got perfect posture. You can walk. Let's begin…

Firstly, I want you to stand opposite your partner, facing each other, and walk towards each other until your bodies are touching. Obviously not nose to nose or toes to toes, which can be rather unnerving! You should be slightly off set, with the lady on the right of the man and maintaining contact with a right front to right front connection, with contact being made at the rib cage. Essentially it's right breast touching right breast, but I usually like to phrase it more diplomatically than that! Your hands should be relaxed and – for the moment – hanging down by your sides.

Even if you are an experienced dancer, this forthcoming exercise is the most important one that you can do to improve your Foxtrot and dancing in general, so please don't just turn the page thinking that you can already do it. Top-class dancers do this regularly, because it's not just good for beginners, it's also the best way for a couple to move more smoothly together and can improve that flow of movement immensely. It's this flow of movement that makes a Foxtrot a Foxtrot!

From standing with each other, as described above (in dancing position, but with your arms down), starting with the man's right foot and lady's left foot, simply walk across the floor maintaining the

position of body contact at all times. It's not as easy as it sounds and a tip from me – the key to this is to roll the body weight through your foot. For the man going forwards it would be from the heel through to the ball and onto your toes (feel the three stages). Therefore for a lady it's toe, then ball and onto your heel. If you're going backwards (sorry girls!) here's the tricky bit – you have to delay the lowering of your heel until your other foot passes it! By doing this you keep your body weight in the perfect place across your foot and your body in contact with your partner. But don't feel left out boys – the roles are reversed and you have to do the same when the lady's walking forwards. It is a simple walking exercise!

When you're walking forwards, you should be in line with your partner (whether you're the man or the lady). For the uninitiated, that means that the man walks forward with his right foot between the lady's feet, whilst the lady steps back with her left foot. As the man places his left foot forwards, he's automatically on the outside of the lady's right foot as she steps backwards onto it. It's a great idea to keep practising this walk as it's the best way of finding your balance with your partner.

You'll never get to be a good dancer with 'bad' feet, so this particular exercise – especially paying attention to your feet now – will help you with every single dance in this book. If you can begin to perfect this walking action, you'll then start to experience how it feels to be a dancer. It's this sensation of perfect harmony with your partner that, for me, is the beauty of ballroom dancing. I would go so far as to suggest that the individual steps of a dance whilst important are less relevant than the feeling of pure synchronised movement.

Putting it simply, if you can't walk together, you can't dance together.

Now that you've mastered the harmony in your partnership, we're going to introduce a third person into this marriage. You. Your partner. And the music makes three. Or rather it makes four, as it's in 4/4 time. That's four even beats per bar of music. The problem is, in the basic step patterns of the Foxtrot, there's only three steps! So, you guessed it, you've got to make three steps fit into four beats. Therefore the rhythm that we give to this is slow-quick-quick. It works in such a way that the slow count has two beats and the quick counts have one beat. So we have slow for one-two, quick-quick for three-four.

Don't worry that the quick beat means you need to go quickly, this is the slow Foxtrot after all. The tempo of the music you'll be dancing to will be 30-32 bars per minute. Can I suggest that you start with *Fly me to the Moon*, Sammy Davis Junior's *Bye Bye Blackbird* or *Let ther be love* by Nat King Cole?

Foxtrot is all about the timing. Therefore, it's the quality of movement across that bar of music combined with the accuracy of timing for the slow, quick-quick rhythm to a one, two, three, four count throughout the dance that becomes the real talent and beauty of a Foxtrot dancer.

I've found that the usual root of any trouble with the Foxtrot is with the slow count. Taking one step over those two beats, and timing the movement of your body weight from your standing leg onto the moving leg, are key to getting it right. Unfortunately it's a matter of practice makes perfect. Mastering the walking

exercise will give you a real advantage here, as you'll gain a greater sense of timing your weight in motion.

So now you just need to know where to put your arms and feet. Personally, I don't believe it's a good idea to over-choreograph the Foxtrot as you lose the character and the beauty of the dance. This is a very flowing dance and the basic step is based on a walking pattern, with an open striding step. In fact, the steps of the Foxtrot haven't actually changed much since its early development. So this means that more importance is laid on your style, movement, balance and timing.

For the actual dance, your body position is exactly the same as it was for the walking exercise earlier, right front to right front. However, I'll finally let you bring those arms up from your sides! Now, this isn't unique for the

Foxtrot – it's actually the same for all the dances apart from the Tango.

The man's right hand is placed on the lady's left shoulder blade with his elbow held up just below the level of his shoulder, giving a slight slope. His left arm is held up, bending the arm at the elbow with his left hand holding the lady's right hand in his. Both of his elbows should be at the same level height. For you ladies, you'll have your right hand in the man's left hand with a bent left elbow. You should have your left hand placed on the upper part of the man's right arm, with your arm on top of his and your palm just below his shoulder. See the picture on page 17 for a little visual guidance.

Feather step

I know I go on about it, but transferring weight is so important, as demonstrated here. The Feather Step starts facing diagonally to centre and can be followed by the Reverse Turn or Three Step.

Ideas for a basic dance sequence

Feather Step, Reverse Turn,

Three Step, Natural Turn, Feather Step,

Natural Turn, Feather Step, Open

Telemark, Outside Swivel, Weave,

Three Step, Natural Turn

STEP 1
Man Step forward right foot, fully transferring weight

Lady Step backwards left foot, fully transferring weight

STEP 2

Man Step forward left foot, in preparation to step outside partner

STEP 3

Man Step forward right foot, outside partner

Lady Step backwards right foot, fully transferring weight

Lady Step backwards left foot, fully transferring weight

Reverse turn

The Reverse Turn is an Open Turn and a Feather Finish, with the lady making a heel turn. It must be danced facing diagonally to centre (see page 14).

STEP 1
Man Step forward left foot, turning to the left

STEP 2
Man Step to the side right foot, continuing to turn

STEP 3
Man Step backwards left foot

Lady Step backwards right foot, turning to the left

Lady Close left foot to right foot, turning from right heel onto left foot (heel turn)

Lady Step forward right foot

STEP 4
Man Step backwards right foot

STEP 5
Man Step to the side and slightly forward left foot

STEP 6
Man Step forward right foot, outside partner

Lady Step forward left foot, turning left

Lady Step to the side and slightly backwards right foot

Lady Step backwards left foot

Three step

This can be danced forwards or backwards and is used to link a feather movement to a natural turning movement. It can be danced along the line of dance or diagonally to centre.

STEP 1
Man Step forward left foot

Lady Step backwards right foot

STEP 2
Man Step forward right foot

STEP 3
Man Step forward left foot

Lady Step backwards left foot

Lady Step backwards right foot

Natural Turn

Start this figure facing diagonally to the wall. It is usually danced from a 3 step. It is a very good figure to dance at a corner followed with a Feather Step.

STEP 1

Man Step forward right foot, turning right

Lady Step backwards left foot, turning right

STEP 4

Man Step backwards left foot, turning right

Lady Step forward right foot, turning right

STEP 2
Man Step to the side left foot

Lady Close right foot to left foot, turning from left heel to right heel (heel turn)

STEP 3
Man Step backwards right foot

Lady Step forward left foot

STEP 5
Man Take a small step to the side right foot, turning from heel of left foot to right foot (heel pull)

Lady Lady Step to the side left foot

STEP 6
Man Step forward left foot

Lady Step backwards right foot, having brushed to left foot

Open Telemark

The Open Telemark is a step that ends in an open position (Promenade Position), and also has a heel turn for the lady. It can be danced from the Feather Step (see pages 22–23).

STEP 1
Man Step forward left foot, turning to the left

Lady Step backwards right foot, turning to the left

STEP 2

Man Step to the side right foot, still turning

STEP 3

Man Step to the side left foot in a Promenade Position

Lady Close left foot to right foot, turning from right heel onto the left foot (heel turn)

Lady Step to the side right foot in Promenade Position

Open natural turn and outside swivel

This figure can be preceded by the Open Telemark and can be danced facing diagonally to the wall in Promenade Position.

STEP 1
Commence in Promenade Position, Man standing on left foot and Lady standing on right foot

STEP 2
Man Step through onto right foot in Promenade Position

STEP 3
Man Step to side left foot, back in front of your partner

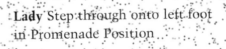

Lady Step through onto left foot in Promenade Position

Lady Step forward right foot, between man's feet

STEP 4
Man Step backwards on right foot

STEP 5
Man Step backwards left foot, lady stepping outside her partner

Lady Step forward left foot

Lady Step forward right foot, outside your partner, closing left foot to right foot, swivelling on right foot into Promenade Position, without changing weight, which remains on your right foot

Weave

This can be commenced in either closed or Promenade Position. Here it is shown from the Promenade Position and can be preceded by the Outside Swivel.

STEP 1
Man Step forward right foot in Promenade Position

Lady Step forward left foot in Promenade Position

STEP 4
Man Step backwards left foot, partner outside

Lady Step forward right foot, outside partner

STEP 5
Man Step backwards right foot

Lady Step forward left foot

STEP 2

Man Step forward left foot, turning left

Lady Step backwards right foot, turning left

STEP 3

Man Step backwards right foot, still turning

Lady Step to the side left foot

STEP 6

Man Step to the side and slightly forward left foot

Lady Step to the side and slightly backwards right foot

STEP 7

Man Step forward right foot, outside partner

Lady Step backwards right foot, partner outside

Originally danced to ragtime music, today the Foxtrot is played by the big bands. It is attributed to the American Vaudeville star, Harry Fox, who had had a career in the circus and as a professional baseball player before being hired to sing in the Vaudeville theatres of San Francisco and from thence on to New York. He danced there on the roof of the converted theatre Jardin de Danse with the Dolly Sisters and, downstairs, unable to find female dancers able to do the more difficult two-step, he introduced two 'trots' and his dance was known as Fox's Trot – like the Turkey Trot and the Onestep it involved trotting. Then it was to a slightly faster tempo than we know now, up to 40 bars per minute and closer to a Quickstep time. American society quickly adopted the Foxtrot, glad to be not dancing animal dances – the Turkey Trot, the Bear Trot, the Possom Trot, the Lobster Trot... what else is a fox if not an animal? I hear you ask. And the famous dance couple, Vernon and Irene Castle, made the Foxtrot elegant, smooth and gliding.

England adopted the Foxtrot and what an incredible sight the London society hotels must have been in the 20s and 30s. The Savoy Hotel was host in their glamorous ballroom to the first slow Foxtrot competition in 1925, which was won by Frank Ford and Josephine Bradley – pioneers of modern Ballroom dancing. Thanks to them, soon after their win, the Slow Foxtrot became a standardised dance to the slow tempo that we now know and the faster version became the Quickstep. Fred Astaire is of course one of my all-time greats – how fabulous! And the biggest selling Foxtrot disk is *Rock around the Clock Tonight* by Bill Haley and His Comets, with reputed sales of 30 million copies.

The flexibility of the Foxtrot, with its quick and slow steps, has made the dance one of the most popular and enduring of all of them. If you can dance the Foxtrot then you can dance any dance.

National Symphony Ball held in the Grand Ballroom Willard Hotel.

The Rumba

If you are ready to feel sexy, then you're ready for the Rumba!

In the first chapter, I spoke about the Foxtrot and the amazing feeling of harmony you can achieve dancing with a partner in Ballroom dancing. For me, it's one of my favourite things about Ballroom dancing. And it's also one of the main draws for me with this Latin dance – the Rumba. It's a very intimate, sexy, sensual dance and you can achieve all of this very easily. So, we can get on with the good stuff rather than just worrying about the steps!

Now that you've mastered your Ballroom Posture, you're all up close and personal, and you will still need that perfect posture for the Rumba. However, having said all that about intimacy and sexiness, Latin dances don't have the same closeness of bodies that Ballroom dances do. In fact, bodies don't touch in the basic hold as they do in Ballroom. So where does that intimacy and the sexiness I've been talking about come in, if there's no body contact? It's in the eye contact. And the hips, but more on those later! In Latin dancing we look at each other! As opposed to ballroom dancing where the heads are turned to the left.

It's such a lovely feeling, dancing the Rumba. Being a slow dance, you have the time to really get involved with both the dance and your

partner! I hope you'll have a flavour and a sense of this by the end of this chapter.

Let's get started: Firstly, you and your partner need to be standing up and facing each other. You should be close enough for the man to place his right hand just beneath the lady's left shoulder blade, but your bodies aren't touching as they are for Ballroom as I explained earlier (see page 20). The man's left hand holds the lady's right hand at shoulder height. And there should be more of a soft curve in your elbows than with the Ballroom hold. The lady's left hand is placed on the man's upper right arm. This is called the closed hold.

Now, although I don't want to get ahead of myself here, there's also an open hold. The open hold once again is opposite and apart from your partner, the man's right hand is completely free, and held out to the side – parallel to the floor and at right angles with the body (this looks nicer than having it by your side, which is not quite as artistic, and you know how I like to be a bit artistic!). Ladies, your left hand is the free one, again with my fabulous artistic position! The man's left hand is holding the lady's right hand in his palm.

Here are some little exercises, but they are an integral part of the dance. So no cheating and trying to take short cuts to the end of the chapter! We'll do one exercise in open hold and one in closed hold.

For the open hold exercise, it's a similar idea to how we approached the Foxtrot – walking backwards and forwards, however, the BIG difference with the Latin walk, compared to that of the Foxtrot walk is that instead of walking forward with your heel leading, here in the Rumba, you'll be stepping forward with the ball of your foot leading. So rather than the heel to the flat movement of the Foxtrot, which you've mastered, this has a ball (of the foot) to flat movement. In Rumba, the heel never leads.

Stand facing each other in your open hold. Fellas, you're walking forwards to start with and ladies you're walking backwards. Starting with the man's left foot going forwards (ladies, your right foot is going backwards), all I want you to do is walk. Your only physical point of contact is the hand hold and you will be able to feel everything that your partner's doing through this connection. Well, that's when he's doing it right! The key is to ensure you don't disconnect your body with the message you're giving through your arm and this exercise will help you to tune in with that feeling.

You should be able quite quickly to achieve a sense of togetherness. Your two bodies should be moving across the floor harmoniously, and the movement is controlled by the man – simply with that one hand.

Now, walk as far as you want before changing and going in the opposite direction. You need to concentrate on controlling that transition. You'll know if you're doing it correctly, guys, as the ladies will be able to tell you! If the movement is fluid and the transition is smooth then you will have an overwhelming feeling of sexiness. If it's a jerky and stilted movement then it's just not

sexy! And if it's just not sexy·it's not Rumba!

For the closed hold exercise, again you're starting off standing and facing each other, this time in the closed hold. Fellas, your weight should be on your left foot here, and ladies need their weight on their right foot. That means you both have a light and free foot available to use.

Here we go then, starting with you men, take your right foot and move it to the side. At the same time the ladies need to move their left foot to the side. It should be about shoulder breadth from your other foot, and then you need to transfer your weight to that foot (the right one for the guys and the left one for the girls).

Leave your other foot where it was, but make it free of your weight. That becomes your new free, available foot which can move forward for the boys and back for the girls (that's your left one, gents, and your right one, ladies). Now, when you do this you should allow your leg to sweep under your hip and end up in front of you, more in line with your hip and no longer out at one side.

You fellas then need to transfer your weight onto your front foot – and onto the back foot for you ladies. You want your heel of your back foot to come off the floor here, gents, and ladies, your heel will be lifted on your front foot.

Feel sexy yet? Just wait!

Now, continue this by replacing that weight back onto your right foot (for the fellas) or left foot (for the ladies). Then step the other foot to the side so you're where you were when we started.

Now I want you to repeat the whole exercise, but I'd like you the man to start off going backwards and the lady forwards. Essentially you're doing it in reverse.

So now you have done the exercises, you know how to walk, find harmony and move those feet! It's time to get a little bit sexier and introduce the hip action!

For the Rumba, the music is a simple 4/4 time, that's four beats to a bar. One-two-three-four. And the tempo is around 30 to 32 bars per minute. The unique thing about the Rumba is that you don't step on the first beat in the bar, just on the two-three-four. The first beat? Well, that's where the hips come in! That's your beat for the hip movement and you move your feet on the two/three/four.

Xavier Cugat was a famous 1920's Latin American band leader and one of the originators of popular Latin American music, and was nick-named the 'Rumba King'! A classic song to dance to is *Bésame Mucho* by Consuelo Velázquez. A favourite song of mine that I danced to with Lesley Garrett is *You'll Never Find Another Love* by Michael Buble.

So that hip action? Well, it's a sideways movement of the hips. Remember that we don't step on the first beat or 'one' count in the Rumba? Well, we still have to do something and that something is with our hips. It's technically called a settlement, but that doesn't sound very sexy now, does it? You're shifting your hips onto the standing leg. Have a look at the pictures of the dance. You've pretty much danced the steps for the Rumba in the closed hold exercise, apart from the hips.

George Raft with Carole Lombard during the filming of *Rumba*

Forward and back basic

Start with the man facing the wall. Normally the Rumba starts with this figure. Step 1 is on beat 2.

STEP 1
Man Step forward left foot

STEP 2
Man Replace weight onto right foot

STEP 3
Man Step to the side left foot

Lady Step backwards right foot

Lady Replace weight onto left foot

Lady Step to the side right foot

Ideas for a basic dance sequence

Forward and Back Basic, New York x 3, to the left, to the right, Spot Turn

to the man's right, Hand to Hand x 3, Spot Turn

STEP 4
Man Step backwards right foot

STEP 5
Man Replace weight onto left foot

STEP 6
Man Step to the side right foot

Lady Step forward left foot

Lady Replace weight onto right foot

Lady Step to the side left foot

New York

The New York can be danced both to the left and the right.

STEP 1

Man Step forward left foot in the left side position

Lady Step forward right foot in the left side position

STEP 2
Man Replace weight onto right foot

STEP 3
Man Step to the side left foot, turning to face your partner

Lady Replace weight onto left foot

Lady Step to the side on right foot, turning to face your partner

The Fan

The Fan starts with a Forward Basic and is followed by a Hockey Stick or an Alemana.

STEP 1
Man Step forward left foot

STEP 2
Man Replace weight onto right foot

STEP 3
Man Step to the side left foot

Lady Step backwards right foot

Lady Replace weight onto left foot

Lady Step to the side right foot

STEP 4
Man Step backwards right foot

STEP 5
Man Replace weight onto left foot

Lady Step forward left foot

Lady Step backwards right foot, turning left

STEP 6
Man Step to the side right foot
Lady Step backwards left foot

Hockey Stick from Fan

The Hockey Stick turns to the left for the lady, from the Fan. The man has to be aware of staying close to the lady when she turns left.

STEP 1
Man Step forward left foot
Lady Close right foot to left foot

STEP 2
Man Replace weight onto right foot
Lady Step forward left foot

STEP 3
Man Close left foot to right foot

STEP 4
Man Take a small step right foot, behind left foot

STEP 5
Man Step forward left foot

Lady Step forward right foot

Lady Step forward left foot, turning left

Lady Step backwards right foot, turning left to face your partner

Spot turn

The Spot Turn can follow the New York or Hand to Hand and can be danced to the left and the right.

STEP 1

Man Step forward left foot (left side to right side position), then turn right to end with right foot in front

Lady Step forward right foot (right side to left side position), then turn left to end with left foot in front

STEP 2

Man Replace weight onto right foot

STEP 3

Man Step to the side left foot, facing your partner

Lady Replace weight onto left foot

Lady Step to the side right foot, facing your partner

Alemana

The Alemana turns to the right from the Fan and can end in closed position.

STEP 1
Man Step forward left foot
Lady Close right foot to left foot

1

STEP 2
Man Replace weight onto right foot
Lady Step forward left foot

2

Rumba

3

STEP 3
Man Close left foot to right foot
Lady Step forward right foot, starting to turn right

STEP 4
Man Step backwards right foot
Lady Step forward left foot towards man, left side still turning right

4

5

STEP 5
Man Replace weight onto right foot
Lady Step forward right foot, away from your partner, still turning

STEP 6
Man Step to the side right foot
Lady Step to the side left foot to face your partner

6

53

Cucaracha

The foot pattern of the Cucaracha shows the transference of weight from the left foot to the right.

STEP 1
Man Step to the side right foot

Lady Step to the side left foot

Going the other way...

STEP 4
Man Step to the side left foot

Lady Step to the side right foot

STEP 2
Man Replace weight onto left foot

Lady Replace weight onto right foot

STEP 3
Man Close right foot to left, changing weight

Lady Close left foot to right, changing weight

STEP 5
Man Replace weight onto right foot

Lady Replace weight onto left foot

STEP 6
Man Close left foot to right, changing weight

Lady Close right foot to left, changing weight

Opening out

1

The Opening Out can be danced from the Spot Turn or Alemana and can be followed by an underarm turn.

Starting from the Closed Position (top left)

STEP 1
Man Step to the side left foot
Lady Step backwards right foot, turning right into open position

2

STEP 2
Man Replace weight onto right foot
Lady Replace weight onto left foot

3

4

STEP 3
Man Close left foot to right foot
Lady Close right foot to left foot, facing partner

STEP 4
Man Step to the side right foot
Lady Step backwards left foot, turning left into open position

5

6

STEP 5
Man Replace weight onto left foot
Lady Step forward right foot

STEP 6
Man Close right foot to left foot
Lady Close left foot to right foot, facing partner

History

The Rumba grew up in Cuba. At times it was an exhibition dance rather than a participation one. It stole from the Contradanza during the nineteenth century, danced in the nightspots of Havanna. Alcedes Castellanos, a Cuban bandleader, is credited with taking the dance to Paris in the 1920s. Like so many of the other Latin dances, the Rumba is a big melting pot of dances, rhythms and flavours from so many places – again largely influenced by the negro slaves taken to Cuba from West Africa and Spain.

The UK was introduced to the Rumba in the 1930s when Monsieur Pierre Margolie went over to learn the dance and add it to his repertoire, and the Square Rumba was presented at the Café De Paris in London, in 1932. It was the famous French demonstrators, The Chapouls, who can be credited with that performance and, having danced the Rumba myself with BBC's *Strictly Come Dancing*'s Tess Daly at the end of series party, I can tell you exactly how grateful I am to them!! The Square Rumba differed from the modern day version – it meant moving your feet on beat one. The rhythm was also different: slow-slow-quick over four beats in the bar. So instead of one-two-three-four, it's one one/two, one one/two, one. And the hip action and the hold were very different too.

A year later, in 1933, Don Azpiazu came to London and brought true Rumba music with him. London's leading dance teacher at the time was Monsieur Pierre and he greeted the Rumba with much enthusiasm (he should also have tried doing it with Tess then!) and his passion for the dance took him and Doris Lavelle to Cuba after the Second World War, where people where dancing Systemo Cubana Rumba, rather than the style seen at the Café De Paris in 1932. He returned with the new way of dancing it... which was widely adopted and became the official, recognised version in the 1950s. The straight-legged technique we dance today then evolved from that of the 1960s and is commonly known as the International Technique.

In the US, heartthrob George Raft played the part of a smooth, sophisticated dancer in the movie *Rumba* directed by Marion Gering in 1935. He won the love of an heiress by dancing, and though an reasonably good dancer, the dancing was mostly done by Frank Veloz. It made the Rumba the most popular dance in America for a while.

The Rumba may be the slowest of the Latin dances, but it's also the most difficult, helping to sharpen sense of rhythm, timing and muscle control. So, if you can master the Rumba, the other Latin dances will come easily.

World Ballroom Dancing Champions Bob Henderson and Eileen Henshall give a demonstration of the Rumba during the BBC's *Television Dancing Club*.

The Waltz

You probably don't expect to hear a Ballroom dance compared to an underwear drawer, but the Waltz is just that. It really IS like your underwear drawer – you can just throw everything in! Choreography-wise I mean. Unlike the Foxtrot, which shouldn't be over-choreographed, the Waltz is a BIG dance – big turns, spins, great big sways and over sways. It's an opportunity to really experiment and to develop figures and timings, yet the elegant foundations of the dance remain throughout.

However, the Waltz doesn't start out as that and, as with so much, you have to start out at the beginning. Learning to dance the Waltz can feel somewhat slow and old-fashioned when you're learning and you can end up feeling as though you're not doing very much. Have you ever watched The Muppets? Animal is the mad drummer in the Muppets. Think of how he waves his arms around and hits all the drums and cymbals. However, in order to get to be the mad drummer, at the start he'd have to sit there with one drum, one stick – just going tap-tap-tap. It takes time and patience to get to be an 'Animal' on the drums. And the same is true of learning to be an animal dancing the Waltz.

I'll try to make it as much fun as possible and I can assure you that it's worth the patience and perseverance needed. When I started to dance the Waltz I enjoyed it first of all, but went through a

real phase of thinking that I couldn't stand it! Before too long I discovered how much there is to get out of dancing the Waltz. As I mentioned earlier, there's just so many different things which you can do and it's really worthwhile starting the journey. However, bear in mind that you do need to start off slowly and build up to the big, swinging swaying movements.

The Waltz is steeped in tradition, but you'll find that it doesn't feel old-fashioned. Whilst it's the original Ballroom dance, and full of grace and elegance, it's a dance that's classical yet modern. So persevere with that tap-tap-tap with one stick on the drums and soon you'll be unleashed!

Here's an exercise to get you into the feel of dancing the Waltz. It's just three little steps – how hard could it be? Clearly, that's just a rhetorical question!

Firstly, starting off, let me remind you about posture and body position. Stand in front of your partner, with your bodies touching right front to right front. Do you remember that from the Foxtrot earlier in the book? Good. Again, take hold – once again the same normal Ballroom position (see pages 12–13).

Now, here's what I want you to do. For the men, you're stepping forward with your right foot; it's just a straight step, by the way. Exactly the same

as you take everyday – the same step you took when you walked into a shop and bought this book (thank you!). At the same time, ladies, I'd like you to step backwards with your left foot. Simple, eh?

So now, the man's weight is on his right foot, and the lady's is on her left foot. For the next step you're going to step to the side. So men, step to the side with your left foot. Ladies, you are stepping to the side with your right foot. At the same time you're transferring your weight onto that foot.

For the third step, you're closing your feet. So boys, close your right foot to your left and girls you're closing your left foot onto your right. It takes you back to the starting position. Three steps over three beats. I told you that it was easy.

Now, all you need to do is repeat this. The boys will start by putting their left foot forward this time and the girl's will start with their right foot going back. So a simple step for beat one. Then take a step to the side for beat two, that's boys stepping with their right foot and girls with their left. For the third beat you're closing the step, so that's left foot to right foot for the boys and right foot to left foot if you're a girl. Again, you're back to where you started. Now, you're ready to use the right foot for the boy and left foot for the girl.

The most important part to remember with the steps here is never to use the same foot twice. You're always transferring weight and then using the other foot. It sounds obvious when you say it, but it is harder to put into practice. Just remember that it's like walking – you don't use the same foot twice when you walk and nor do you when you waltz.

Whoever I'm dancing with – Lesley Garrett, Patsy Palmer, or whoever it may be next series – I'll always start off with them on this exercise. Unless you can change weight correctly from one foot to the other in this exercise, I'm afraid the Waltz will be impossible.

In my experience, the biggest problem that people encounter is starting off with the same foot twice in a row. I don't know why this is, but it seems that it's so easy to forget which foot has just been used at the end of step three. The memory of which foot it was is wiped in an instant! So just try to keep in mind this rule about not using the same foot twice. You should be able to cheat your memory slightly and keep on track of the correct feet by slightly lifting the heel of the foot which you're about to use at the end of step three. Then you'll notice that it feels ready to use when you're finishing up that third step and ready to take step one again.

Now, one major characteristic of the Waltz, which we need to talk about is the rise and fall. Rise and fall certainly isn't unique to the Waltz. However, it's the rise and fall in this dance which gives it elegance. Forgive me if you already know about rise and fall but, even if you think that you do, it never hurts to refresh your memory. Perhaps you know about rise and fall from the other Ballroom dances, which they all have? Bear in mind that it is far more pronounced in the Waltz than with the others because of the closing of the feet in step three – which you did in our earlier exercise.

Rise and fall isn't about the steps – it's about the footwork. Have a think about how you normally use your feet when you walk. You would start on your heel and then go onto the flat of your foot when taking a step. That's a simple walking action. Now, the girls as going backwards – again thinking of the simple walking action – although walking backwards. Your foot would start on your toe and then go back onto the flat of your foot, wouldn't it? Again, it's based on a walking action, the same as the Foxtrot – do you remember that walking exercise from the Foxtrot? You've perfected that one, so this one should be a doddle! Honest.

Now, let's do the exercise we did above but now start to think about the rise and fall. The first step is just as in when you walk, going from heel to flat foot – or toe to flat foot if you're going backwards. Then for the second step, the step to the side, you step to your toe and stay lifted up on your toe. So when you close the step by bringing your feet together you will have both feet on their toes with your heels off the ground. At the very end, you lower back down again and start all over. Now, the closing up and the lowering are both on beat three. You don't stay up, you get yourself to up and then lower immediately. It may sound rather bizarre and complicated but it's really quite natural when you actually do it.

Now, you have the exercise we did earlier and I want you to do it, simply walking up and down the floor. Firstly all the way up, and then on the way back the boys will have to go backwards. Then I'd like you to repeat it, but adding in that rise and fall. And before you know it·you'll be Animal from the Muppets!! (That's a compliment, I promise!)

The music for a Waltz has a slower and more melancholic feel and that's because of the timing. It's 3/4 time, which is three even beats to a bar. I've always thought that even the word Waltz conjurers up a picture of something rather old-fashioned, don't you agree? The melancholic music fits right into this for me –

think about how something like *Moonriver* by Danny Williams has that feel – rather than a brighter 4/4 time piece of music. Now, don't assume that just because a piece of music is melancholic that it will fit the Waltz, it does have to be the more unusual 3/4 timing – as there are only three steps, and there are many pieces of slow music in 4/4 or other timings.

On the very first show on the very first series, Lesley Garrett and I danced the Waltz to a piece of music called *He Was Beautiful*. It was quite a significant moment to take to the dance floor the very first time in the series – we could only hope and anticipate what a success the show might become. Oh, and did I mention that we got the top marks on that show! Oh well, sadly one swallow doesn't make a summer does it? Now when I look back fondly to the heady start of the first series it seems all too brief and distant!!

Natural turn

The Natural Turn is so called because it turns to the right; any turn to the left is called a reverse turning variation. Commence facing diagonally to the wall and end diagonally to the centre.

STEP 1
Man Step forward right foot

STEP 2
Man Step to the side left foot, turning right

STEP 3
Man Close right foot to left foot

Lady Step backwards left foot, turning right

Lady Step to the side right foot

Lady Close left foot to right foot

Ideas for a basic dance sequence

Natural Turn, change step, Reverse Turn, Whisk into a Chassé

STEP 4
Man Step backwards left foot, turning to the right

STEP 5
Man Step to the side right foot (shown here without turn, to show foot position)

STEP 6
Man Close left foot to right foot

Lady Step forward right foot, turning to the right

Lady Step to the side left foot, still turning to the right (shown here without turn, to show foot position)

Lady Close right foot to left foot

Reverse turn

Commence the Reverse Turn facing diagonally to centre and end facing diagonally to the wall. This step can be followed by a Whisk and a Chassé.

STEP 1
Man Step forward left foot, turning left

STEP 2
Man Step to the side right foot, still turning

STEP 3
Man Close left foot to right foot

Lady Step backwards right foot, turning left

Lady Step to the side left foot

Lady Close right foot to left foot

STEP 4
Man Step backwards right foot, turning left

STEP 5
Man Step to the side left foot (shown here without turn, to show foot position)

STEP 6
Man Close right foot to left foot

Lady Step forward left foot, turning left

Lady Step to the side right foot, still turning to the left (shown here without turn, to show foot position)

Lady Close left foot to right foot

Whisk

The Whisk can be followed by a Chassé. It is normally danced facing the wall.

STEP 1
Man Step forward left foot

Lady Step backwards right foot

STEP 2

Man Step to the side right foot

STEP 3

Man Cross left foot behind right foot, opening partner into Promenade Position

Lady Step to the side left foot

Lady Cross right foot behind left foot, turning into Promenade Position

Chassé

The Chassé is normally danced from a Whisk but
it can be danced from any figure that ends in the
Promenade Position.

STEP 1
Man Step forward right foot in
Promenade Position

STEP 2
Man Step to the side and slightly forward left foot

Lady Step forward left foot, in
Promenade Position

Lady Step to the side right foot, starting to turn to
face partner

STEP 3
Man Close right foot to left foot

STEP 4
Man Step to the side and slightly forward left foot, preparing to step outside partner

Lady Close left foot to right foot, facing partner

Lady Step to the side right foot

Spin turn

The Spin Turn has a pivoting action for the man and a brushing action for the lady. It commences with the first three steps of a Natural Turn.

STEP 1
Man Step backwards left foot, pivoting on it to the right (keeping right foot in front of you)

Lady Step forward right foot, pivoting on it to the right

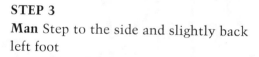

STEP 2

Man Step forward right foot, still turning to the right

Lady Step backwards left foot, still turning, and brush right foot to left foot

STEP 3

Man Step to the side and slightly back left foot

Lady Step forward right foot, diagonally

Weave

The Weave commences from Promenade Position facing diagonally to the centre, ending either in the Promenade Position or closed position – whichever the man decides to lead.

STEP 1
Man Step forward right foot, in Promenade Position

STEP 2
Man Step forward left foot, turning left

STEP 3
Man Step to the side and slightly backwards right foot, turning left

Lady Step forward left foot, in Promenade Position

Lady Step to the side and slightly backwards right foot, turning left

Lady Step to the side and slightly forward left foot, turning left

STEP 4
Man Step backwards left foot, outside partner

STEP 5
Man Step backwards right foot

STEP 6
Man Step to the side left foot in Promenade Position

Lady Step forward right foot, outside partner

Lady Step forward left foot

Lady Step to the side right foot, in Promenade Position

Weave (feet only)

The Weave feet positions, showing both the Promenade ending and the Closed ending

STEP 1
Man Step forward right foot, in Promenade Position
Lady Step forward left foot, in Promenade Position

STEP 2
Man Step forward left foot, turning left
Lady Step to the side and slightly backwards right foot, turning left

STEP 3
Man Step to the side and slightly backwards right foot, turning left
Lady Step to the side and slightly forward left foot, turning left

STEP 4

Man Step backwards left foot, outside partner
Lady Step forward right foot

STEP 5

Man Step backwards right foot
Lady Step to the side left foot, still turning to the left

STEP 6A Promenade end

Man Step to the side left foot, in Promenade Position
Lady Step to the side right foot, in Promenade Position

STEP 6B Closed end

Man Step to the side and slightly forward left foot, turning left
Lady Step to the side and slightly backwards right foot, turning left

History

The English Waltz, developed much later than the Viennese Waltz and, whilst both are rotational dances, it's important not to confuse them. We'll come to the Viennese Waltz later in the book. All the historical references to the Waltz are really about the Viennese Waltz, as opposed to the English Waltz – as we do it today – which didn't really start until the 1920s and was originally called the Diagonal Waltz. Victor Sylvester won the first World Championships for Waltzing in 1922, dancing a more simple series of steps than we have today. The English Waltz evolved after the star championships were held in London in 1927, at a time when dance trends and fashions were changing; the Imperial Society of Teachers of Dancing was looking to standardise the Waltz. They announced that whoever won the competition would set the standard by whichever version of the Waltz they danced – and it was the diagonal Waltz that the winners danced (those two most elegant and talented dancers, Alex Miller and Phyllis Haylor) – and so that is what became the version that was danced as standard – the English Waltz. However, the dance was popularised way before that – despite early shock at the scandal of two people dancing so closely together it soon transpired that Queen Victoria, who was an excellent ballroom dancer, had a special affection for the Waltz and so it became acceptable within society.

Above: Ballroom dancing in the 1950s.
Right: Queen Victoria and Prince Albert take to the dancefloor.

Cha cha cha

The first dance I teach anyone who wants to learn a Latin American dance is the Cha Cha Cha. It really is a fun dance, with such lively music and a quicker tempo. It's one of those dances that give you a great uplifting feeling inside. You'll also discover that it has a melting pot of styles and rhythms, all going on at the same time – which gives a great sense of freedom. But, most importantly, with the Cha Cha Cha you feel as if you are dancing from the moment you begin to learn it, rather than simply reciting the steps.

Personally, I like to be a bit mischievous when teaching this dance. I'll explain more about the timing in a moment but, because of the way that the timing works, it works well as a dance to play around with and perhaps move shoulders or hips instead of taking a step. Isn't it great to get to do something with your body that you wouldn't normally do – all in the good name of dancing?!!

So you know that feeling when the radio's on at home and a great song comes on and so you start dancing around the kitchen because no one's looking? Well, with the Cha Cha Cha it's exactly the same sense of vibrant gay abandon! Oh – just make sure that your window cleaner doesn't catch you!! As that old Irish proverb says, 'Work like you don't need money, Love like you've never been hurt, And dance like no one's watching'. Let's get you started then.

Stand facing each other, as with the Rumba. That's opposite each other and not touching each other. Your hands are in a double hand hold – which means that you're holding each others hands – with the palms facing your partner, not the floor or ceiling.

The man stands with the weight on his right foot and his left foot – the free leg – out to the side. Ladies, you have your weight on your left foot and your free foot is out to the side – mirroring your partner. We are starting this on the second beat in the bar – not the first – this begins on the two count. So for this beat – I'd like you to close your free foot to the foot you're standing on and transfer the weight over. So boys you're then standing with the weight on your left and the ladies have their weight on their right foot (your feet are still next to each other). Now, for beat three, you simply transfer your weight back over again to the original foot (boys – left and girls – right). For the fourth beat, boys will step to the side with their left foot and transfer weight to that left foot. Leave your right where it was, without weight on it. Girls, you're mirroring your partner by stepping to the side with your right foot and transferring your weight – and both of you need to remember to transfer your weight completely. Now I'd like you to close your feet again – that's boys bringing your right foot to the left and girls bringing your left foot to the right. This is the 'and' count (Think: two, three, four

AND one, two, three, four etc) before going back into beat one. For beat one, the boys step to the side with their left foot, and girls step to the side with their right and once again both of you need to remember to transfer your weight over completely.

Now, I promised earlier that I'd explain how the timing works for this dance and, although we've just touched on it, brace yourself now for the technical bit! The timing for this dance starts on the second beat of the bar. So we begin on the two count of a one-two-three-four timing. The dance has a complete beat for two, and a complete beat for three, but the fourth beat is actually two half beats. That's why it becomes the 'and' that I spoke of earlier. So it's actually two-three-four and-one-two-three-four-and etc. It might make more sense if you think of it in this way two-three-CHA CHA CHA. two-three-CHA-CHA-CHA. The Cha Cha Cha part is the four and one part of the timing. It's actually how the dance got its name – the ladies' shoes would make that cha cha cha noise on the floor when dancing those beats. I do believe that makes the dance onomatopoeic!! Good word, eh? That's the technical bit over, it wasn't too exhausting was it?

Now the point of this exercise is to get a real feeling of the rhythm of the dance being THE single most important thing about it. Also, while you're doing this exercise with your partner, you will get to feel that changing of weight between you and this will help you to stay in harmony, a really key part of dancing with a partner. Despite the fact that our bodies aren't touching, just our hands, it's essential that we're moving together. This exercise will give you an opportunity to concentrate on the transfer of weight in the dance, without overwhelming yourself early on with steps and choreography.

One of the biggest problems with this dance is finding yourself on the wrong foot. This usually isn't because you've done a wrong step, as you might expect, but actually can often be because you've changed the rhythm. So you could have left a step out and ended up with your weight on the wrong foot. Or perhaps you've not transferred your weight correctly. If you can do the right rhythm and transfer your weight properly, then you'll always be on the correct foot. I've included this exercise – which I show everybody that I teach first – because it's designed to get you to change weight properly, keep rhythm and attain harmony with your partner.

There's such an eclectic array of songs which suits this dance. It has a 4/4 rhythm (four beats per bar, regardless of us starting on the second beat) – with a quicker tempo than the Rumba. You could try Basement Jaxx's *Red Alert* or *Bingo Bango*, or *Sway* by Michael Buble.

1950 *Que Lindo Cha Cha Cha!* movie poster

Forward basic

Forward and Back Basic is the beginning of the Cha Cha Cha and
from here everything else follows.

STEP 1
Man Step forward left foot

STEP 2
Man Replace weight onto
right foot

Lady Step backwards right foot

Lady Replace weight onto
left foot

STEP 3
Man Step to the side left foot

STEP 4
Man Close right foot to left foot

STEP 5
Man Step to the side left foot

Lady Step to the side right foot

Lady Close left foot to right foot

Lady Step to the side right foot

Back basic

STEP 1
Man Step backwards right foot

STEP 2
Man Replace weight onto left foot

Lady Step forward left foot

Lady Replace weight onto right foot

Cha cha cha

STEP 3
Man Step to the side right foot

STEP 4
Man Close left foot to right foot

STEP 5
Man Step to the side right foot

Lady Step to the side left foot

Lady Close right foot to left foot

Lady Step to the side left foot

New York

The New York can be danced both to the left and to the right. It is preceded by the Forward and Back Basic.

STEP 1
Man Step forward left foot in the left side position

STEP 2
Man Replace weight onto right foot

Lady Step forward right foot in the left side position

Lady Replace weight onto left foot

STEP 3
Man Step to the side left foot, facing your partner

STEP 4
Man Close right foot to left foot

STEP 5
Man Step to the side left foot

Lady Step to the side right foot, facing your partner

Lady Close left foot to right foot

Lady Step to the side right foot

Hand to hand

The Hand to Hand can be danced both to the left and to the right
and can be preceded by a Forward and Back Basic or a Spot Turn.

STEP 1
Man Step backwards right foot,
in the left side position

STEP 2
Man Replace weight onto
left foot

Lady Step backwards on the left
foot, in the left side position

Lady Replace weight onto
right foot

STEP 3
Man Step to the side right foot, facing your partner

STEP 4
Man Close left foot to right foot

STEP 5
Man Step to the side right foot

Lady Step to the side left foot, facing your partner

Lady Close right foot to left foot

Lady Step to the side left foot

Basic to Fan

The Basic to Fan is followed by the Hockey Stick or the Alemana.

STEP 1
Man Step forward left foot
Lady Step backwards right foot

STEP 2
Man Replace weight right foot
Lady Replace weight left foot

STEP 6
Man Step backwards right foot
Lady Step forward left foot

STEP 7
Man Replace weight left foot
Lady Step to the side and slightly backwards right foot

STEP 3
Man Step to the side left foot
Lady Step to the side right foot

STEP 4
Man Close right foot to left foot
Lady Close left foot to right foot

STEP 5
Man Step to the side left foot
Lady Step to the side right foot

STEP 8
Man Step to the side right foot
Lady Step backwards left foot

STEP 9
Man Close left foot to right foot
Lady Cross right foot in front of left foot

STEP 10
Man Step to the side right foot
Lady Step backwards left foot

Hockey stick
from fan

STEP 1
Man Step forward left foot
Lady Close right foot to left foot

STEP 2
Man Replace weight onto right foot
Lady Step forward left foot

In this figure, when the lady turns left, the man must not be too far away from her, so keep close and don't lose contact!

STEP 6
Man Place right foot behind left foot in a small step
Lady Step forward left foot

STEP 7
Man Step forward left foot
Lady Step forward right foot, turn to the left and face your partner

STEP 3
Man Small step to the side onto the left foot
Lady Step forward on the right foot

STEP 4
Man Close right foot to left foot
Lady Cross left foot behind right foot

STEP 5
Man Step to the side left foot
Lady Step forward right foot

STEP 8
Man Step forward right foot
Lady Step backwards left foot

STEP 9
Man Cross left foot behind right foot
Lady Cross right foot in front of left foot

STEP 10
Man Step forward right foot
Lady Step backwards left foot

Alemana
from fan

STEP 1
Man Step forward left foot
Lady Close right foot to left foot

STEP 2
Man Replace weight onto right foot
Lady Step forward left foot

1

This is a turn to the right for the lady. You will find this is much easier if you take the 5th step of the Fan (lady's right foot stepping forward) towards the man.

STEP 6
Man Step backwards right foot
Lady Turning to the right, step forward left foot under the arm to the man's left side

STEP 7
Man Replace weight onto left foot
Lady Continuing to turn right, step forward right foot away from your partner

6

7

STEP 3
Man Take a small step to the
side left foot
Lady Step forward right foot

STEP 4
Man Close left foot to right foot
Lady Cross left foot behind
right foot

STEP 5
Man Step to the side left foot
Lady Step forward right foot,
starting to turn right

STEP 8
Man Take a small step to the
side right foot
Lady Step to the side left foot,
turning to face your partner

STEP 9
Man Close left foot to right foot
Lady Close right foot to left foot

STEP 10
Man Step to the side right foot
Lady Step to the side left foot

Spot turn

The Spot Turn can be danced to the left or to the right, preceded by the New York or the Hand to Hand.

STEP 1
Man Step forward left foot in left side position, then turn right to end with right foot in front

STEP 2
Man Replace weight onto right foot

Lady Step forward right foot in left side position, then turn left to end up with left foot in front

Lady Replace weight onto left foot

STEP 3
Man Step to the side left foot to face your partner

STEP 4
Man Close right foot to left foot

STEP 5
Man Step to the side left foot

Lady Step to the side right foot to face your partner

Lady Close left foot to right foot

Lady Step to the side right foot

Backward lock step (feet only)

The Lock Step must be danced with the heel of the back foot staying off the floor during the lock section (the crossing section). The three steps of the Lock are used as the cha cha cha when travelling forward and backwards, so when you move to the side it's a Chassé and when you move backwards it's a Lock.

STEP 1
Man Step forward left foot
Lady Step backwards right foot

STEP 2
Man Replace weight onto right foot
Lady Replace weight onto left foot

STEP 3
Man Step backwards left foot
Lady Step forward right foot

STEP 4
Man Cross right foot in front of left foot
Lady Cross left foot behind right foot

STEP 5
Man Step backwards left foot
Lady Step forward right foot

Forward lock step (feet only)

STEP 1
Man Step backwards right foot
Lady Step forward left foot

STEP 2
Man Replace weight onto left foot
Lady Replace weight onto right foot

STEP 3
Man Step forward right foot
Lady Step backwards left foot

STEP 4
Man Cross left foot behind right foot
Lady Cross right foot in front of left foot

STEP 5
Man Step forward right foot
Lady Step backwards left foot

Forward and back basic

This is just a reminder of the foot pattern for the Forward Basic for the man and the Back Basic for the woman. A simple step but so important and, as ever, don't forget to change weight!

STEP 1
Man Step forward left foot
Lady Step backwards right foot

STEP 2
Man Replace weight onto right foot
Lady Replace weight onto left foot

STEP 3

Man Step to the side left foot
Lady Step to the side right foot

STEP 4

Man Close right foot to left foot
Lady Close left foot to right foot

STEP 5

Man Step to the side left foot
Lady Step to the side right foot

Shortly after slavery was abolished in Cuba in 1886, the US occupied Cuba for six years until 1904. Dance flourished with the ex-slaves merging their traditions with those of the Spanish and local islanders. From the Danzon and the Son came the Mambo, a dance originating in Haiti, 'mambo' being the name of a Voodoo priestess used by the slaves brought from West Africa in their religious practices. And from that the Cha Cha Cha developed before the Second World War. It was a Triple Mambo, there being also a Single and a Double Mambo, with the name Cha Cha Cha coming from the scuffing sounds of the girls' feet on the floor. The name is onomatopoeic. It refers also to the three hip movements that make up the Cha Cha Cha.

On one of his several visits to Havana, in 1952, the leading British dance teacher Pierre Lavelle observed that the Rumba was being danced with extra beats and when he returned to Britain he started to teach this new dance. With the 1953 recording of the Cuban composer and violinist Enrique Jorrin's *La Enganadora* (1948) and especially with Perez Prado's *Cherry Pink And Apple Blossom White* (1955), the Cha Cha Cha became hugely popular both in the US and Britain. It was fast, it was fun. Its origins are firmly with the negroes of West Africa. And by the mid 1950s the Cha Cha Cha, along with the Merengue and the Rock 'n' Roll, was danced everywhere.

Arthur Murray simplified it to make it easier and slower. Minon Mondajar is credited with introducing the dance to the US and, amongst the Latin dances, Cha Cha Cha was unique in being danced to music with voices singing. One of the early steps was called the 'chatch', which was three quick changes of weight preceded by two slow steps. Movies were made featuring the dance – *Qué lindo Cha Cha Cha*, *The World of Suzy Wong*, and *Cha Cha Cha Boom* being well worth seeing. Walter Laird is responsible for the modern form of Cha Cha Cha, developed in the 1960s, which is danced today in competitions the world over. It is the most recent of the Latin dances.

Perez Pantalon Prado, king of the Cha Cha Cha, demonstrates the Cuban dance with Gisele Robert in Paris in 1955.

The Tango

The Tango is a distinctive dance. It's romantic and dramatic, a little bit exotic (I like the sound of it already), very simple and yet absurdly tricky. The Tango has become a familiar dance in popular culture – unlike most Ballroom dances – I bet nearly everyone you know could describe something about it because it has a story, a vibrancy, an intensity that people find attractive. The Tango is one of the classic Ballroom dances but it is a dance of passion with its roots firmly founded in Latin America. Tango is the story of the gaucho, the woman of the night and the dimly lit seedy salons of Argentina. The men are looking for entertainment from the women and the women are looking for payment.

In modern Tango the men are less sweaty and the women not paid for their wares so readily, but the passion remains. Ballroom Tango is deeply influenced by the Argentine Tango but is different and should not be confused because it is a more progressive dance. The story and backbone of the Ballroom dance are inherited from the Argentine Tango and it takes all the wonderful Latino tricks into the Ballroom style. Tango has a unique place in the world of Ballroom dancing because of the passion and intensity that make the dance work. You have to feel the Tango to be able to do it.

The Tango is easily identified as it has become familiarised in popular culture. What is the Tango itself? It is a dance of two parts. There is the progressive part of the dance, like all Ballroom dancing, where you move around the floor, but you also have the tricky swivels and flicks that are more stationary. As a dancer you are constantly trying to integrate these two parts of the structure and character of the dance. You get the best of both worlds with the Tango. The flicks, swivels and tricks of the Argentine Tango make it inventive and fun to dance whilst the Ballroom style of progressing around the floor gives it that romantic feeling.

As with all other Ballroom dances, the feeling of harmony between the couple is tantamount. Not being in harmony in the Tango has an added sense of danger, as you will learn when you have kicked you partner fourteen times in the shins. The man has to be confident in his movements and really lead the lady with the feel of complete togetherness. I must add that even though togetherness is the most important factor in all Ballroom dances, it somehow seems more crucial in the Tango than any other.

I want you to try this little exercise before you take on any of the swivels and slightly more adventurous kicks. Boys, stand in your slightly offset position, in front of your partner but slightly to the right-hand side of you, so you should be right front to right front touching. Now the hold is slightly different in the Tango. Boys take hold of the girl's right hand, pick up the arm to the man's eye level – at this point it's the same as the Foxtrot – but for the Tango you need more of a bend in the elbow with the hands coming in towards the couple. The man's right arm goes around the lady's back, slightly lower than the shoulder blades, with the man's fingers crossing the lady's spine. The reason for this is so that the lady can place her left hand over and

The sensuous world of the tango is explored in United Artists' drama *Assassination Tango*.

underneath the man's arm with the palm facing down, as opposed to placing the hand on top of the arm like in the Foxtrot. The feeling of this hold is that the man has gathered the lady in with the hold being much more compact. The lady should feel a longer contact through the body – a slightly more intimate position – you can see why I like the Tango so much.

Now boys, you are going to step forward with your left foot. Girls, you are going to step backwards with your right foot. Boys, then step forward with your right foot and girls you are going to step backwards with your left foot so we have literally just done two walks. At this point, I can't emphasise enough that the person going backwards must take a large step because if you take a small step the person coming forward may step on your toe, which never really shows passion in my mind, and it causes a disharmony in the progression of the weight going from foot to foot. You get what we call a banging walk where you keep bumping into each other – not what we want to see. Just imagine all this can be solved by taking a large step. How simple is that?

From there, with the man standing on his right foot with his left foot behind him so the weight has been transferred to the right foot, and the lady standing on her left foot with her right foot in front of her but the weight transferred to the left foot, they rock from foot to foot, transferring the weight but not closing the feet. So men, rock backwards onto your left foot, then rock forward onto your right foot and then rock backwards again onto your left foot. Ladies, obviously do the natural opposite. So it is three movements. From there boys, step backwards onto your right foot, fully transferring your weight. Always remember to transfer weight, never be in no man's land, neither Arthur nor Martha you shall be. At this point in time the lady has stepped forward onto her left foot. Then together you step to the side, on the man's left foot, lady's right foot, then once you've stepped to the side, having transferred weight, close your feet (man closes right foot to left foot, the lady left foot to right foot). Even though you have closed your feet (you've got it!) you must transfer your weight back – onto the man's right foot and lady's left foot – so you are ready to start the exercise again. Fantastic. Once you've done this exercise a few times, the key thing to develop here in order to help you with your Tango and to get a sense of the style is to take long enough steps so you can change weight comfortably. Boys, it's your job to lead the lady to transfer weight through your movement, so you must have complete control over your movement – it must be strong, unwavering and clear to your partner which direction you are travelling in, whether rocking your feet or taking a step to move into a new position. The moment you can make these things clear to your partner and she can do them comfortably without hesitation, you are on your way to the Tango and a little bit of passion.

I remember dancing the Tango with Patsy Palmer in Series 3 of *Strictly Come Dancing*, and it was our best week. I've got lot of stories about not winning with the judges, but I digress... The reason it was such a successful dance for us is that we were able to harmonise through the character and music of the dance, so the steps didn't cause us a problem and we could go out and express our enjoyment of the dance. When we came to Tango week, we started on the first day of training with this exercise to get our

bodies and our weights moving together. This enabled us to build into the dance and we came together very simply and quickly. Because of the longer contact with the body you can feel what's going on and feel the body weight of your partner moving so you can follow in a more instinctive fashion. Just to reiterate, it is so important that the man is sure and strong in his movement from foot to foot and positive in his weight transferences and it's essential for the lady to give in to the man and feel the dance coming through his body.

The music of the Tango is written in 2/4 time but 4/4 time is often used. The tempo is about 33-34 bars per minute. The Tango music has a distinct character and flavour. Carlos Gardel and Astor Piazzolla are the famous Tango composers and musicians that made Tango music so popular. In June 1935 a Cuban woman committed suicide in Havana and a woman in New York and Puerto Rico poisoned themselves all over the same man who none of them have ever met. This man was Tango composer Carlos Gardel who had just died in a plane crash in Colombia. Almost single-handedly he took the style out of the Buenos Aries tenements and bought it to Paris. It was said of Astor Piazzola and his Tango music, that if they were to shoot a capsule onto the moon with five pieces of music in it that sum up music on earth, his would be one of them.

It's important not to confuse Argentine Tango music with Ballroom dancing music because the tempo can be a bit slow or variable so the Argentine music is often used but played at a strict tempo.

Left foot walk

STEP 1

Man Step forward left foot, fully transferring weight

Lady Step backwards right foot, fully transferring weight

Right foot walk

STEP 2

Man Step forward right foot, fully transferring weight

Lady Step backwards left foot, fully transferring weight

Progressive link

STEP 3
Man Step forward left foot
Lady Step backwards right foot

STEP 4
Man Short step to the side and slightly back, with right foot opening to Promenade Position
Lady Short step to the side with left foot turning into Promenade Position.

Ideas for a basic dance sequence

Start with left foot walk into Rock Turn, link to Closed Promenade, Five step,

Outside Swivel – and start again

Closed promenade

STEP 1
Man Step to the side left foot, in Promenade Position

STEP 2
Man Step through with right foot, in Promenade Position

Lady Step to the side right foot, in Promenade Position

Lady Step through with left foot, in Promenade Position

Tango

STEP 3
Man Short step to the side left foot
Lady Short step to the side right foot

STEP 4
Man Close right foot to left foot
Lady Close left foot to right foot

Five step

The Five Step consists of four steps, but for the fifth step we have a turning promenade with the weight remaining left foot for the lady, right foot for the man. It is very important the lady steps outside her partner on step 3 with her right foot. It commences facing diagonally to wall.

STEP 1
Man Step forward left foot

STEP 2
Man Step to the side and slightly backwards right foot

STEP 3
Man Step backwards left foot, partner outside

Lady Step backwards right foot

Lady Step to the side and slightly forward left foot

Lady Step forward right foot, outside partner

STEP 4
Man Step backwards right foot

STEP 5
Man Turn into Promenade
Position, remaining on right foot

Lady Step forward left foot

Lady Turn into Promenade
Position, remaining on left foot

Reverse turn

The Reverse Turn can be danced facing diagonally to centre and end diagonally to wall. It can be followed with a Progressive Link, Five Step or any variation that starts on the left foot.

STEP 1
Man Step forward left foot, turning left

STEP 2
Man Step to the side left foot, still turning

STEP 3
Man Step backwards left foot, partner outside

Lady Step backwards right foot, turning left

Lady Step to the side and slightly forward left foot, still turning

Lady Step forward right foot, outside partner

STEP 4
Man Step backwards right foot, turning left

STEP 5
Man Take a small step to the side left foot

STEP 6
Man Close right foot to left foot

Lady Step forward left foot, turning left

Lady Step to the side right foot

Lady Close left foot to right foot

Reverse turn (feet only)

STEP 1
Man Step forward left foot, turning left

Lady Step backwards right foot, turning left

STEP 4
Man Step backwards right foot, turning left

Lady Step forward left foot, turning left

STEP 2
Man Step to the side left foot, still turning

Lady Step to the side and slightly forward left foot, still turning

STEP 3
Man Step backwards left foot, partner outside

Lady Step forward right foot, outside partner

STEP 5
Man Short step to the side left foot

Lady Step to the side right foot

STEP 6
Man Close right foot to left foot

Lady Close left foot to right foot

Pivot turn for promenade position

A more advanced figure can be preceded by a progressive link.
Continuing to turn through Steps 2, 3 and 4 is vital to achieve
this step.

STEP 1
Man Step forward left foot, in
Promenade Position
Lady Step forward right foot, in
Promenade Position

STEP 2
Man Step forward right foot, in
Promenade Position
Lady Step forward left foot, in
Promenade Position

STEP 3
Man Step to the side, facing
partner, turning right
Lady Step forward right foot,
between the man's feet

STEP 4
Man Step forward right foot,
turning left
Lady Step to the side left foot,
turning left

STEP 5
Man Step backwards left foot
Lady Step forward right foot

STEP 6
Man Step backwards right foot
Lady Step forward left foot

5

6

STEP 7
Man Step to the side left foot
Lady Step to the side right foot

STEP 8
Man Close right foot to left foot
Lady Close left foot to right foot

7

8

Outside swivel from promenade position

The Outside Swivel has a very characteristic feel of the Tango and is preceded by any variations that ends in Promenade Position – ie. Progressive Link or Five Step.

STEP 1
Man Step forward left foot, in Promenade Position

STEP 2
Man Step forward right foot, in Promenade Position

STEP 3
Man Step forward left foot

Lady Step forward right foot, in Promenade Position

Lady Step forward left foot, in Promenade Position

Lady Step to the side right foot, turning to closed position

STEP 4
Man Step forward right foot, outside partner

STEP 5
Man Step backwards left foot, tapping right foot across, without weight

STEP 6
Man Step forward right foot, tapping left foot to the side without weight

Lady Step backwards left foot, flick right foot in front of left foot

Lady Step forward right foot, swivelling to end in Promenade Position, remaining on right foot

Lady Step forward left foot in Promenade Position, swivelling to end in closed position, remaining on left foot

Natural rock turn (with a left foot walk)

The Rock Turn can be commenced diagonally to the wall or along the line of dance. A nice figure to start with.

STEP 1
Man Step forward left foot
Lady Step backwards right foot

STEP 2
Man Step forward right foot
Lady Step backwards left foot

1

2

STEP 3
Man Step to the side and slightly backwards left foot
Lady Step to the side and slightly forward right foot

STEP 4
Man Rock forward onto right foot
Lady Rock backwards onto left foot

3

4

STEP 5
Man Rock backwards onto left foot, small step
Lady Rock forward onto right foot, small step

STEP 6
Man Step backwards right foot
Lady Step forward left foot

5

6

STEP 7
Man Step to the side left foot
Lady Step to the side right foot

STEP 8
Man Close right foot to left foot
Lady Close left foot to right foot

7

8

History

'Come let's make a date
To Tango quite late,
And when we get tired
We'll just Hesitate'

The Tango grew out of the Argentine Tango, a dance developed in Buenos Aires by the West Indian and Cuban immigrants imitating the dances of the negroes from Africa. By the 1870s it was popular throughout Argentina and Uruguay. Originally called the Milonga, the gauchos, who wore chaps, got caked in sweat from their horses' bodies and went to the clubs seeking girls at the end of the day; the ladies – they held their heads

back when dancing to avoid the smell but they made money and were happy! The great writer Jorge Luis Borges says, 'Tango belongs to the Rio de la Plata and it is the son of Uruguayan "milonga" and grandson of the "habanera"'.

The Argentine Tango grew in popularity, and was danced by society in Brazil. Early in the twentieth century, dancers and musicians from South America travelled to Europe and the Tango took hold first in Paris and then in Berlin, London and St Petersburg (in London the dance had to be modified with the erotic components toned down). It hit New York just a year before the outbreak of World War I. And by 1914, the 'North American Tango' was styled. The silent movie *Four Horseman of the Apocalypse* released in 1921, exposed Tango to the masses once again as the smouldering Rudolph Valentino took to the dance floor. By 1921 the Tango was standardised at a conference in London.

In the 1930s a German couple came to London to compete in Tango dances with a new interpretation of the Tango. They pushed boundaries and controversially changed the timing as well as the style from a slow fluid dance to a staccato and sharp dance. They developed different ways for the lady to use her head in flicks and positions. They also introduced longer strides and a more progressive style like the other ballroom dances. The landscape of the Tango was changed forever as the two tangos separated and the Ballroom Tango emerged.

More than any other dance, you'll find movies and musicals featuring the Tango. Madonna's *Evita* and *True Lies* with Arnold Schwarzenegger and Jamie Lee Curtis are just two worth watching. And for musicals, there's *Tango Argentino* and *Forever Tango, Tango x 2, Tango Pasion* and many more. As Al Pacino said in the movie *The Scent of a Woman*, 'The Tango's the easiest dance. If you make a mistake and get tangled up, you just Tango on.'

The Paso Doble

The Paso Doble, more than the other Latin dances, is a characterised dance because you are telling the story of an actual moment in time - the Bullfight. The two main rolls that are being portrayed are the matador – strong, dominant, mastering the bullring with the inner steel of a man close to potential death at the horns of a bull; and the cape – strong yet feminine, fluid and receptive to the matador's every whim. The man produces strong body shapes and positions with the lady matching and following his every move to lure the bull towards them and then move out of the way with an arching or turning of the body at the last second. This is a game between man and beast, the matador gracefully using the cape to toy with the bull until that final moment of death – the coup de grâce. The Spanish nature of this dance allows dancers to take on the flair, passion and pride of Spain and, most importantly, get a few of your favourite flamenco steps in there too, with flamenco being an essential ingredient to the nuances and characteristics of the dance.

The dance itself is passionate, vivacious, dramatic – probably the most intense of all the dances in attitude and focus – it's a rather serious dance actually because you have to engross yourself in it to be convincing in your story-telling, otherwise it just looks a bit, well, silly. I love playing the role of the macho matador in the Paso Doble. Of course this could be

something to do with my mother being Spanish; maybe it's in my blood or, maybe it's just because I'm a big show off! I love the drama and the feeling of the scene unfolding. When you're choreographing this dance you have a beginning, a middle and an end and invariably the music has a highlight where it comes to a stop at the coup de grâce – when the bull is killed – and this adds to the excitement and intensity.

Now, because of the nature of the Paso Doble, with its inherent choreographed tradition of a beginning, middle and end, it is usually danced competitively, seldom socially, which is a shame because it is a fabulous and dramatic dance. It's a lovely dance to lead because of the grand shapes and gestures, which we'll talk about later. Now I don't really have an exercise. What I'm going to do is show you a variation that really encompasses the feeling of matador and cape and the march-style movements of the Paso Doble. It's called the Sixteen, simply called this because it's got, well, sixteen steps – see how that works? It must have been the last one they invented that day and they had run out of names by that point...

Now let's talk about the shapes. The shaping of the bodies is important because it creates a strong lead for the lady and also gives the dance the character needed to represent the matador and his cape. The shaping should be an exaggerated movement of the body where you lean to the left

or right with the arms curved over the head allowing the bull to whizz past you. The bodies should be toned, all the way to the fingertips. The need for good shaping and toned bodies is heightened because of the speed of the music – it gets on a bit in the Paso Doble, quickest of all the Latin dances. The main problems occur if you've got a floppy body and your lead isn't strong because then you lose the marching drama of the dance.

The music is a 2/4 count with 60 beats per minute so very quick. Popular music includes *España Cañi* (*Spanish Gypsy*) and *Que Viva España* and the modern Lalo Schrifrin theme music from *Mission Impossible*.

Now we start with the boys. Stand with your feet together, facing your girl and do what we call an Apel, which is a stamp of your right foot on the spot. Don't go mad and start bruising yourself though. Then you step forward with your left foot in Promenade Position (where the man's right side and the lady's left side are towards each other, but slightly apart, and the opposite side of the bodies are turned outwards to form a V shape, whilst maintaining normal hold). Ladies, you do the natural opposite, you do an Apel (both remembering to change one's weight when 'apeling') with your left foot and then step forward with your right foot. Now from there, boys step forward, still in Promenade Position and lady do the same thing with your left foot, maintaining your Promenade Position. Then boys, with your left foot turn to cross the lady's path so that you're facing her, so you are turning to the side, but stepping slightly back to ensure you don't bump into her. At this point, ladies, step forward with your right foot, stepping between the boy's feet. Boys step backwards with your right foot, ladies step forward with your left foot. Boys step backwards with your left foot, ladies step forward with your right foot, outside partner (so just outside his right foot, on his right side). Now this time boys, close your right foot to your left foot and, as you do that, turn to face your girl. Ladies, you take a step to the side with your left foot so you feel like you've just stepped a little bit past him. Boys, you replace weight onto your left foot without a step, so just change weight. Girls, you step back onto your right foot, so replace your weight onto your right foot, leaving your feet apart.

Now, boys, for the last 8 steps you are just marching on the spot, changing weight. Girls, step forward and across the front of the boy with your left foot. Men change weight. Ladies, right foot to the side, then you replace the weight back onto your left foot with your feet apart, then you step forward across the front of your man with your right foot. Boys still standing on the spot, changing weight. Girls, step to the side with your left foot. Then replace weight with your right foot, feet still apart. Left foot forward in front of the man and then you close your right foot to your left foot for the final step, ending facing each other. And at this point, boys, you should have changed weight so that you are back to where you began. Now that's an exercise. What a belter that is. I feel we got a bit technical with outside partner and Promenade Position, but they are both integral parts of Latin and Ballroom dancing and, if you can perfect them, your dancing will come on in leaps and bounds. The easiest way to check this exercise is that the steps should add up to – wait for it – 16. So boys when you're just changing weight, each change of weight is one count. This step is actually quite an advanced step but the

Paso Doble

lovely thing about it is that encompasses the character of the dance with the way the cape (woman) swishes in front of the matador. And also, it introduces you to new positions and it's a very progressive step so, if you get this one right, the Paso Doble will be a piece of cake.

Side steps

A simple step to get into the Paso Doble mood. The arm styling can be danced as shown or in closed hold.

STEP 1
Man Step to the side right foot
Lady Step to the side left foot

STEP 2
Man Close left foot to right foot
Lady Close right foot to left foot

1

2

STEP 3
Man Step to the side right foot
Lady Step to the side left foot

STEP 4
Man Close left foot to right foot
Lady Close right foot to left foot

3

4

Ideas for a basic dance sequence

Start facing the centre, Side steps, Sur Plas x 4 (walking on the spot and turning to the left of the right), Separation, Sur Plas into Sixteen, Sur Plas

---

5

STEP 5
Man Step to the side right foot
Lady Step to the side left foot

STEP 6
Man Close left foot to right foot
Lady Close right foot to left foot

6

7

STEP 7
Man Step to the side right foot
Lady Step to the side left foot

STEP 8
Man Close left foot to right foot
Lady Close right foot to left foot

8

Separation

STEP 1
Man Appel – Close right foot to left foot with a small stamp of the foot
Lady Close left foot to right foot, with a small stamp of the foot

STEP 2
Man Step forward left foot
Lady Step backwards right foot

STEP 3
Man Close right foot to left foot
Lady Step backwards left foot

Paso Doble

5

6

7

8

STEP 4
Man Change weight, leaving left foot in place
Lady Close right foot to left foot

STEP 5
Man Change weight from left foot to right foot
Lady Step forward, small step, left foot

STEP 6
Man Change weight left foot
Lady Step forward, small step, right foot

STEP 7
Man Change weight onto right foot
Lady Step forward, small step, left foot

STEP 8
Man Change weight onto left foot
Lady Close right foot to left foot

Sixteen (1)

The Sixteen commences facing wall and continues down the line of dance. Boys, remember to close your feet on step 7, but allow the ladies to continue.

STEP 1
Man Appel – close right foot to left foot, turning to Promenade Position
Lady Close left foot to right foot, turning to Promenade Position

STEP 2
Man Step to the side foot, in Promenade Position
Lady Step to the side right foot, in Promenade Position

STEP 3
Man Step forward right foot, in Promenade Position
Lady Step forward left foot, in Promenade Position

STEP 4
Man Step to the side and slightly backwards left foot
Lady Step forward right foot

Paso Doble

STEP 5
Man Step backwards right foot
Lady Step forward left foot

STEP 6
Man Step backwards left foot,
lady outside
Lady Step forward right foot,
outside partner

STEP 7
Man Close right foot to left foot
Lady Step to the side left foot

STEP 8
Man With feet together, change
weight from left foot to right
foot
Lady Replace weight onto
right foot

5

6

7

8

Sixteen (2)

STEP 9
Man Change weight onto
right foot
Lady Step forward and across,
left foot

STEP 10
Man Change weight onto left
foot
Lady Step side to side, right foot

STEP 11
Man Change weight onto
right foot
Lady Replace the weight onto
left foot

STEP 12
Man Change weight onto
left foot
Lady Step forward and across
with right foot

STEP 13
Man Change weight onto right foot
Lady Step to the side, left foot

STEP 14
Man Change weight onto left foot
Lady Replace weight onto right foot

STEP 15
Man Change weight onto right foot
Lady Step forwards towards the man, left foot

STEP 16
Man Change weight onto left foot
Lady Close right foot to left foot

Coup de pique (feet only)

Commence the Coup de Pique facing the centre of the room. The first part of the step is an effective way of changing feet.

STEP 1
Man Point right foot forward and across in a Promenade Position
Lady Point left foot forward and across in the Promenade Position

STEP 2
Man Close right foot to left foot
Lady Close left foot to right foot

STEP 3
Man Step backwards with left foot
Lady Step backwards with right foot

STEP 4
Man Close right foot to left foot
Lady Close left foot to right foot

STEP 5
Man Step backwards left foot
Lady Step backwards right foot

STEP 6
Man Step to the side right foot
Lady Step to the side left foot

STEP 7
Man Close left foot to right foot
Lady Close right foot to left foot

STEP 8
Man Step to the side right foot
Lady Step to the side left foot

STEP 9
Man Close left foot to right foot
Lady Close right foot to left foot

4

7

5

8

6

9

History

'Paso Doble' is Spanish for 'Two Step'. The name Paso Doble is not as well known as most of the other Latin dances, but it is very widely performed. It is based on the notion of a bullfight. The man represents the torero (bullfighter), and the woman represents the cappa (cape). The Paso Doble is a form of dance rather than a series of actual steps and the torero tosses, swings and swirls his cappa in every direction. When you see the Paso Doble you would easily recognise it as a Latin dance, but there is no specific time or step, as there is in most Latin dances. It's simply a two step with its own distinct, swinging movement.

Bull worship in Crete was known centuries ago and the cult of the bull spread across Europe. Possibly the Moors and the Christians in the Spanish War of Reconquest, when bored of fighting each other, began to fight wild animals, including the proud bulls on the Iberian peninsula. The first recorded bullfight (corrida) in Spain was at the coronation of King Alfonso VIII in 1133. One Spanish King, Philip II, invoked the Pope's help to ban bullfighting in the seventeenth century. Then Francisco Romero put modern bullfighting on the map a century later and it is on his form of the bullfight that the Paso Doble is based, being performed before the bullfight began.

Andalusians loved the 2/4 time Spanish marching music popular through the eighteenth century. The French Bourbon influence in Spain lingered and there was an infantry march called the 'Pas Redoublé', perhaps the origin of the name and why the dance is always done to strict marching music. Undoubtedly several of the moves in this dance have French names. Whatever, it is the only Latin dance not to have its roots in negro culture.

The Paso Doble became extremely popular in the 1920s and became 'the next thing' in Paris during the years before the Second World War, and this is another reason why many descriptions are in French. Pierre Margolie, the British dance teacher, perfected dances such as the Paso Doble and demonstrated them dancing with Doris Lavelle both in France and England, particularly in London's Greek Street and in the Café de Paris. Today it is not danced in a social arena, but in competitions, though, in Vietnam, some of Western Germany, in France and Spain you can find it danced socially. Of course the Australian movie *Strictly Ballroom* has the Paso Doble as the focus of the storyline. The frocks are gorgeous, I just love them.

The Quickstep

The Quickstep is fabulous, darling. It is one of the most popular Ballroom dances because of its speed and splendour. Like the Tango, you can break down the dance into two parts – the big sweeping movements across the floor and the jumps, hops, tricks and quick steps, which make the dance so exciting and fun to do. It is Erin's favourite dance (probably because she dances it with me!), I'm a bit of a mad quickstepper – all hell breaks loose, in a slightly controlled way. I love the sense of abandonment… in a tail suit.

The Quickstep is a dance that gives you a great sense of elation and, danced well, you feel swept away. It's like you're flying and it can literally take your breath away. I once danced Quickstep in a huge competition. We had made the final and the Quickstep was the last dance. I was feeling tired and emotional and then the music struck up and it was a real favourite of mine and the tune just lifted me. I flew around the floor, spinning, running, skipping, jumping, kicking – it was incredible – I was carried through on a wave of ecstasy and delight. And that is how the Quickstep should make you feel. It's tricky and intricate but the big movements of swishing and spinning across the floor take you away. I love that about it.

The Quickstep was born out of the Foxtrot and they are my two favourite dances. When you dance, you think of energy, vibrancy, excitement and emotion – these words epitomise the Quickstep. It has all the physical components to make you slump down into your chair at the end of it and say, 'that was amazing'. It's a dance you lose yourself in, which makes it so much fun to do. You are always pushing the boundaries of how far you can go without being out of control – you want that feeling of a controlled out of control, if that makes any sense!

The only problem of feeling like you're on a rollercoaster, in the same way a child looks at fireworks, is the anticipation of what is coming next – in the Quickstep you've got to keep your mind in tune so you know what step you are going to do to add that extra something. I am always trying to do a more exciting move, add a new layer, sweeping and turning and kicking and skipping and flying and spinning, but, I'm afraid it's not as easy as it sounds. You have to start from the beginning. As lovely as it is to fly you've got to start on the ground and get your speed up. And sometimes this can take a bit of time. A classic example of what the poet Anton once said, 'You're going to have to learn to walk before you can give it the full bifta!'.

Moving slowly with your partner is tricky enough, but moving quickly with your partner is a whole new galaxy of tricky-ness. Alas, it's one of those boring moments when you really have to learn your steps and take it slowly. The main issue of dancing at speed is trust and you need to build the trust between you and your partner. You've got to dance together and be spatially aware. Once again we come back to having perfect posture – a familiar phrase in the world of Anton Dancing. You don't want to kick your partner half to death, unless his Foxtrot was rubbish and this is payback time!

The rhythm of the Quickstep is slow, quick-quick, slow. We will talk more about the music later. Now, I'm going to give you a little exercise that's going to be very simple. Of course when I say simple, what I mean is once you can do it perfectly, then it's simple. You're going to get the rhythm right yourself, and in harmony with your partner. The key to this is to dance the exercise confidently and in a positive fashion; dance this tentatively and you're going to get hurt, you'll be on the wrong foot and it just won't work – it will all be very disappointing to everybody concerned and fellas, the ladies will adjourn to the powder room to moan about your Quickstep. Being tentative has no place in the Quickstep – stand tall and walk strong.

So, assume the ballroom position of standing in front of your partner with perfect posture. Gentlemen, offer the lady a fabulous bodyline which she can dance with, present a good ribcage which she can place her body against; by doing this she will be fully aware of your weight transference. Men, gather in your ladies, with your right front to right front position and take her in your normal Ballroom hold (man's right hand just under the lady's left shoulder blade, lady's left hand on the man's right arm, on his right bicep and men pick lady's right hand up in your left hand) making sure you give her a good frame, picking your elbows up so she knows you mean Quickstep action. Men, stand facing the wall at the top of the room as you are going to move down the room (obviously with the lady backing the wall). Men step forward with your right foot leading on a strong heel (ladies step back on your left foot) – this is just a normal walking step – on the slow count. Men step your left foot to the side, ladies step your right foot to the side, quick count, completely transferring your weight. Chaps, close right foot to left foot, ladies close left foot to right foot on quick count, once more, you've got it, change your weight. Then boys, step to the side with your left foot, girls with your right foot, for the final slow.

Now, repeat that all over again but the boys start off going backwards on the right foot and the ladies go forward on the left foot. So then men step to the side on your left foot (ladies step to the side on your right foot), then close up the feet (men right foot to left foot, ladies left foot to right). Boys now step to the side with your left foot and ladies with your right foot for the final slow. Now, we are going to repeat from the beginning, but with one slight difference – that the man now steps forward with his right foot but outside his partner: because of the speed of the music he cannot step inline. Now I hear you asking, 'what does outside his partner mean?' I hear your cries and pain and anguish – the prospect of 'outside your partner' is truly frightening – what does this mean? But fear not, it is not as difficult as it sounds, you only have to

step forward on your right foot to the right of the lady's right foot – that's called 'outside of partner'; if I had stepped to the left of her right foot then that would have been 'in line'. If you try to step in line at speed you will kick the lady so step outside and stay happy. Continue this exercise always remembering to maintain your posture, stand tall and keep a good frame. And boys whenever you step forward from this point, step outside your partner. We talk about flow a lot in Ballroom dancing, it's a major component, and this exercise is designed to keep the fluidity of the dance. You've got to master this exercise as though you are flowing across the floor on a cushion of air, without any jerks and bumps; you should get a lovely sense of Quickstep with the body weights moving across the floor – freedom and fluidity – lovely. You don't need to accelerate you just need to let it go… and flow.

I'm going to talk to you about rise and fall. We spoke about this in the Waltz briefly. I'm sorry to get technical on you but like all things, to develop this you must add a new layer, and this is the next layer after your perfect posture and correct hold (I appreciate I might be presuming a bit here but I have great confidence in all of you!). Now comes the step pattern, the rise and fall. As with the Waltz, boys you start forward on the heel, ladies normal backward walking step please. Now you step to the side (boys left foot, girls right foot), going directly to the toe. Join your feet together on toes, and then as you step to the side again for the last slow, onto a toe but directly lower onto the flat foot. Think the 'sl' part of the slow is the toe and the 'ow' part is the foot flat, ready to commence the whole exercise again with the girl coming forwards and boy going back. This may seem all a bit tricky but it's this

Ginger Rogers and Fred Astaire in *The Story of Vernon and Irene Castle*

footwork that enables you to get that all essential fluidity that we talked about earlier. Think of the footwork as the wheels of your beautiful running Rolls Royce or, if you're a bit quicker, something a little more sporty.

The timing of the Quickstep is 4/4 time and the tempo is 50 bars per minute so you can see it's pretty quick. Great Quickstep tunes are *Sing Sing Sing* by Benny Goodman or something more modern would be *Suddenly I See* by Katie Tunstall.

Quarter turn

The Quarter Turn is an important figure. The starting figure of the Quickstep is facing diagonally to the wall.

STEP 1

Man Step forward right foot, turning right

STEP 2

Man Step to the side left foot, continue turning

Lady Step backward left foot, turning right

Lady Step to the side right foot

Ideas for a basic dance sequence

Quarter Turn, Progressive Chassé, Lockstep, Spin Turn,

Progressive Chassé

STEP 3
Man Close right foot to left foot

STEP 4
Man Step to the side left foot

Lady Close left foot to right foot

Lady Step diagonally forward
right foot

Chassé to the right

Chassé to the right commences facing diagonally to the centre, and can be followed by a Back Lock

STEP 1
Man Step forward left foot

STEP 2
Man Step to the side right foot

Lady Step backwards right foot

Lady Step to the side left foot

STEP 3
Man Close left foot to right foot

STEP 4
Man Step to the side right foot

Lady Close right foot to left foot

Lady Step diagonally forward left foot

Lock step

This step is normally danced diagonally to the wall. It can be danced forward or backwards for the lady and man.

STEP 1
Man Step forward right foot, outside partner

STEP 2
Man Step diagonally forward left foot

Lady Step backwards left foot, partner outside

Lady Step backwards right foot

STEP 3
Man Cross right foot behind
left foot

STEP 4
Man Step diagonally forward
left foot

Lady Cross left foot in front of
right foot

Lady Step diagonally backwards
right foot

Lock step (feet only)

STEP 1
Man Step forward right foot,
outside partner

STEP 2
Man Step diagonally forward
left foot

Lady Step backwards left foot,
partner outside

Lady Step backwards right foot

STEP 3
Man Cross right foot behind
left foot

STEP 4
Man Step diagonally forward
left foot

Lady Cross left foot in front of
right foot

Lady Step diagonally backwards
right foot

Natural spin turn

This step commences facing diagonally to wall and has a pivoting action for both man and lady, with the lady also doing a brush step.

STEP 1
Man Step forward right foot, turning right

STEP 2
Man Step to the side left foot, still turning

STEP 3
Man Close right foot to left foot

Lady Step backwards left foot, turning right

Lady Step to the side right foot

Lady Close left foot to right foot

STEP 4
Man Step backwards left foot, pivoting on it to the right (keeping the right foot in front of you)

STEP 5
Man Step forward right foot, still turning

STEP 6
Man Take a small step backwards and to the side left foot

Lady Step forward right foot, pivoting on it to the right

Lady Step backwards left foot, brush right foot to left foot

Lady Having brushed right foot to left foot, step diagonally forward on to it

Spin turn

The Spin Turn commences facing diagonally to the wall and can be danced at the corner of the room. There is a lovely feel of pivoting on steps 4 and 5.

STEP 1
Man Step forward right foot, turning right
Lady Step backwards left foot, turning right

STEP 2
Man Step to the side left foot, still turning
Lady Step to the side right foot

STEP 3
Man Close right foot to left foot
Lady Close left foot to right foot

STEP 4

Man Step backwards left foot, pivoting on it to right foot (keeping the right foot in front of you)
Lady Step forward right foot, pivoting on it to the right

STEP 5

Man Step forward right foot, still turning
Lady Step backwards left foot, brush right foot to left foot

STEP 6

Man Take a small step backwards and to the side left foot
Lady Having brushed right foot to left foot, step diagonally forward on to it.

Running finish

The Running Finish is normally preceded by a Back Lock and is danced down the line of dance.

STEP 1
Man Step backwards left foot, turning right, partner outside

STEP 2
Man Step to the side right foot, still turning

Lady Step forward right foot, turning right, outside partner

Lady Step to the side left foot, still turning

STEP 3
Man Step forward left foot,
still turning

STEP 4
Man Step forward right foot,
outside partner

Lady Step backwards right foot,
still turning

Lady Step backward left foot,
partner outside

Quick open reverse

The Quick Open Reverse is a left turning variation and commences facing diagonally to the centre. It is usually followed by a Chassé.

STEP 1
Man Step forward left foot, turning left

Lady Step backwards right foot, turning left

STEP 2
Man Step to the side right foot, still turning

STEP 3
Man Step backwards left foot, partner outside

Lady Step to the side left foot

Lady Step forward right foot, outside partner

History

The Quickstep was born in New York suburbs during the First World War, when Caribbean and African dancers living in the city developed it. In the 20s it was danced in the American music halls and from thence it graduated to the ballrooms all over the country, much influenced by the social climate. The dances at the time were the Foxtrot, Waltz and Tango. There were also different dances like the Bunny-hug, the Turkey Trot, the Black Bottom, the Shimmy, the Onestep and the Charleston (which have all disappeared into obscurity except for the Charleston, though it is no longer danced much). The big bands were playing Jazz, Ragtime and different types of beat music with new exciting rhythms. With the faster music, dancers had to follow and so new dances were created. The slow Foxtrot sped up, sometimes to as fast as 50 bars to the minute, and took moves from the other dances to create a new dance called the Quickstep. People became so excited by new dances such as the Charleston – Charleston fever really started in 1925 – that in the ballrooms everywhere it became dangerous, with the exuberant masses of arms and legs everywhere and so signs were put up saying 'PCQ' (Please Charleston Quietly) and new rules were strictly enforced for the dancers' personal safety. Somehow it seems a shame that it was restricted so. People would literally pass out from the excitement and vitality of the dance!

Molly Spain and Frank Ford, an English couple, danced the 'Quicktime Foxtrot and Charleston' leaving out the Charleston knee movements, and also danced it as a couple rather than solo, at the 'Star' Championships in 1927. And so it was that in the late 20s the English adopted the Quickstep to replace the 'Quicktime Foxtrot and Charleston' with its quicker tempo and exciting choreography and the Foxtrot was once again the Foxtrot. And the Quickstep became one of the standardised Ballroom dances with the characteristic Chassé steps. It became the most popular dance of the day very quickly. In reality, it is more of a cross between the Waltz and the Charleston, with the ideas of floating across the floor combined with the lighter foot movements of the Charleston.

Today there are international Quickstep competitions all over the world for both professionals and amateurs. The movements are on a grand scale so this requires a larger room than for most of the dances.

Santos Casani dancing at his school in 1931.

The Samba

If you can imagine Carmen Miranda's headdress, her high heel shoes, her exuberance and lust for life, then I give you the Samba. It is like those sweets you put on your tongue and they explode, that's the Samba, it's an explosion of a dance. It's also a cultural dance and a symbol of Brazil. Samba music combines three different cultures: the Portuguese songs, the African rhythms and fast-paced Indian rituals.

During the first series of *Strictly Come Dancing*, in order to tease the Latin dancers I said that the Samba was a bit made up and wasn't a proper dance at all, which made me laugh, the upside was I could rib all the Latin dances, and the downside is that nobody thinks I like the Samba, which isn't the case at all. Contrary to popular belief, I just love its sense of fun. The Samba, for all its energetic and rhythmic movements, quicker tempo music and a sense of 'anything goes', is actually the most difficult of all the Latin dances to perfect. This is basically because of the timing of the movement with the music. I find it amazing that a dance can start as an Afro-Brazilian rhythm, using beats from African prayer and then carry through to become a symbol of Brazil and an embodiment of the carnival. It has grown from one that was danced by slaves to become one that symbolises a culture and a nation.

As I've just mentioned the Samba is the most difficult of all the Latin dances, so you have to take it easy to begin with, because if you rush this dance, although you might get to learn the steps in a hurry, you will never really learn to dance the Samba. It's all about the timing and the changing rhythms. The music is a 2/4 time but the first beat is split between a 3/4 of a beat and then a 1/4 of a beat and then the second beat is a whole beat (one-a-two) so it has what we call a split beat rhythm (i.e. three counts but two beats). Now at this moment in time I'm going to have a little lie down – all that technique has worn me out. I promise that's the last of it. But you've got to get to grips with the rhythm because you know what they say, rhythm is… a dancer.

There are two progressive dances in the Latin fold – the Paso Doble and the Samba. Although you do move in the other Latin numbers you don't progress around the floor, like Ballroom dances.

Here we go then. I'm going to give you a little exercise. This little exercise is actually the first steps you should learn, but they are so good to learn as an exercise that I'm going to show you them as well, because you can get the whole essence of the Samba from these few steps. What we are going to do is start off with a few stationary

steps but they will give you a lovely idea of the dance and its rhythm.

Boys, stand in front of your partner in normal Latin hold with your right hand on her back and your left hand holding her right hand with a space between your two bodies (so you're not touching through the body). Boys I want you do to something for me, step forward for count one on your left foot, girls step backwards on your right foot. Boys, you're going to close your right foot to your left foot and girls close your left foot to your right foot for the 'a' count. Then step onto the other foot (boys left foot, girls right foot) with your feet remaining together so it's just a change of weight. Now, you've achieved that, well done. You have to repeat that with the man stepping backwards on the right foot and the girl stepping forward on her left foot, for step one. We then continue the process, so boy closing left foot to right foot, girl closing right foot to left foot, for the 'a' count. And then transferring your weight back to right foot for boys, left foot for girls for count two. So you now find yourself exactly where you were when you started. If you're not then it means you haven't changed weight correctly somewhere along the exercise. So the best thing to do is stop and start again with the man's left foot. I want you to repeat this exercise four times. And then we're going to move into the second part of the exercise, which links straight onto the end of the forward backward part. At the end of it boys you should have your left foot available, all those of you have their left foot available say 'I', even those of you at the back who wish you were doing the Quickstep, and give yourself a pat on the back.

Chaps, you're going to the side now, with your left foot, not forward or backward, but to the side. Ladies step to the side with your right foot on the count 1. With our right foot boys, 'we've changed our weight here haven't we boys – yes Anton'. Boys, take your right foot and do a whisk action, now what does that mean eh? Boys, cross your right foot behind your left foot and transfer weight. Girls cross their left foot behind their right foot and transfer weight – this is on the 'a' count. Now replace the weight back to the left foot for the boys and back to the right foot for the girls for the 2 count. Now we repeat the same action but going the other way so, boys step to the side on your right foot and girls step to the side on your left foot. Then boys this time whisk your left foot behind your right foot (so the crossing action we just discussed) and girls whisk your right foot behind your left and then replace the weight back onto the boys right foot and girls onto their left foot for the two count. Just keep remembering one-a-two, one-a-two. Now you should be back where you started with your left foot available boys and your right foot available girls. And I want you to repeat this whisking exercise four times. Now you need to join the exercises together so you start off with your forward and back basics and then link straight into your side whisks. By this point you should start to feel the rhythm of the dance.

The most important thing to remember and the most problematic thing is one in the same, summed up in one word – yes, you've got it, it's the timing. The Samba does have a bit of a bounce to it, but I don't want to talk about it too much otherwise everyone will go mental and go bouncy bouncy bounce. It's a controlled bounce contained within the legs and hips... but we will come to

that later. Firstly, let's get the timing going.

The samba music is 2/4 time. A bit like all 2/4 time you can get away with using 4/4 time, but obviously I didn't say that. To all you muso's out there, I do know it's different. A few great tunes are *Mas Que Nada* – one of my favourites – *Brasil* and *Love is in the Air*.

Forward and back basic step

STEP 1
Man Step forward right foot

STEP 2
Man Close left foot to right foot

STEP 3
Man Change weight onto right foot

Lady Step backwards left foot

Lady Close right foot to left foot

Lady Change weight onto left foot

Samba

Ideas for a basic dance sequence

Forward and Backward Basic Step, Whisk,

Samba Walk, Whisk

STEP 4
Man Step backwards onto
left foot

STEP 5
Man Close right foot to left foot

STEP 6
Man Change weight onto
left foot

Lady Step forward onto
right foot

Lady Close left foot to right foot

Lady Change weight onto
right foot

Whisk

The Whisk can be danced both to the left and the right and is preceded by forward and back basics.

STEP 1
Man Step to the side left foot

STEP 2
Man Place right foot behind left foot

STEP 3
Man Change weight onto left foot

Lady Step to the side right foot

Lady Place left foot behind right foot

Lady Change weight onto right foot

STEP 4
Man Step to the side right foot

STEP 5
Man Place left foot behind right foot

STEP 6
Man Change weight onto right foot

Lady Step to the side left foot

Lady Place right foot behind left foot

Lady Change weight onto left foot

Samba walk

This step can be commenced in the Promenade Position and can be followed with the Whisk.

STEP 1
Man Step forward right foot in Promenade Position
Lady Step forward left foot in Promenade Position

STEP 2
Man Step backwards left foot in Promenade Position
Lady Step backwards right foot in Promenade Position

STEP 3
Man Slide right foot slightly back
Lady Slide left foot slightly back

1

2

3

STEP 4
Man Step forward left foot in Promenade Position
Lady Step forward right foot in Promenade Position

STEP 5
Man Step backwards right foot in Promenade Position
Lady Step backwards left foot in Promenade Position

STEP 6
Man Slide left foot slightly back
Lady Slide right foot slightly back

4

5

6

Volta cross

The Volta movement is a travelling figure, which can be followed by the Whisk or Botafogo.

STEP 1
Man Step to the side left foot

STEP 2
Man Step across in front of left foot with right foot

Lady Step to the side right foot

Lady Step across in front of right foot with left foot

Samba

STEP 1
Man Step to the side left foot

STEP 4
Man Step across in front of left
foot with right foot

Lady Step to the side right foot

Lady Step across in front of
right foot with left foot

Botafogo in closed position

When you're doing the Botafogo you must remember that the step to the side is what we call a 'part weight transference', so you don't transfer the weight fully and allow the heel to go down – it's not often I say that!

STEP 1
Man Step forward and across right foot

STEP 2
Man Place left foot to the side

STEP 3
Man Replace weight onto right foot

Lady Step backwards and across left foot

Lady Place right foot to the side

Lady Replace weight onto left foot

STEP 4
Man Step forward and across left foot

STEP 5
Man Place right foot to the side

STEP 6
Man Replace weight onto left foot

Lady Step backwards and across right foot

Lady Place left foot to the side

Lady Replace weight onto right foot

Botafogo in shadow position

STEP 1
Man Step forward and across left foot
Lady Step forward and across left foot

STEP 2
Man Place right foot to the side
Lady Place right foot to the side

STEP 3
Man Replace weight onto left foot
Lady Replace weight onto left foot

STEP 4
Man Step forward and across right foot
Lady Step forward and across right foot

STEP 5
Man Place left foot to the side
Lady Place left foot to the side

STEP 6
Man Replace weight onto right foot
Lady Replace weight onto right foot

2

3

5

6

History

In the 1670s the Portuguese discovered a place in South America that they called the January River (Rio de Janeiro). As their settlement there grew, slaves from Angola and the Congo were brought in to work in Bahia, in the north east of what became Brazil. Their African rhythms were used in their homeland to call forth various gods (Samba means to pray or to invoke your personal god/saint) in dances such as the Caterete, the Batuque and the Embolada, and these were transported and enveloped into the Latino music. The Batuque, with its steps similar to the Charleston, and done to the beat of hand clapping and the sounds of percussion, became so popular that the Emperor Manuel I outlawed it. The native dances, which involved the touching of navels, were seen as sinful by the Europeans and were often suppressed. These religious African rhythms heavily influenced the dance of today, making it a unique genre of music. The name Samba may come from Zambo, the word used to describe the child of a native Brazilian woman and an African man, or it may come from the Bantu word meaning to invoke the spirit of your ancestors.

In the 1830s the African slaves had mingled with the local Lundu peoples and a composite dance was developed which joined the plait figures of the Negro dances with the body rolls and sways of the Brazilians. Carnival steps were gradually included. But then the dancers began to hold each other in the European way (closed dance position) and the high society of Rio made it 'the latest thing' and at this stage it was known as the Zemba Quecca. It then modified into the Mesemba. At the turn of the nineteenth century, the Mesemba was combined with the Maxixe, which was popularised in the US and Europe. Once it was danced in Paris, it instantly became the rage and the Samba as danced today still uses a step called the Maxixe.

In the 1930s a form of Samba called the Carioca was danced in the UK and this dance was introduced into US in 1939 by Carmen Miranda. When the Samba was performed at the World Exhibition in New York in 1939, it really took off. Movies such as *Flying down to Rio* with Fred Astaire and Ginger Rogers, and Carmen Miranda, in her many films, including *That Night in Rio*, gave the Samba huge popularity and also at this time many Latin American bands like Tito Puento popularised the music adding to the flavour and excitement of this Latin American dance. One of the best exponents of the Samba in England was Walter Laird who, with his partner Lorraine, developed the dance considerably.

Like the Paso Doble, it is a progressive dance and is performed all over the world in competions as well as being a social dance. And of course it is always a centrepiece at the Rio Carnival held forty days before Easter to mark the beginning of Lent, where the Samba schools, founded in 1928, parade around the streets in glorious extravagance.

Sao Paulo Carnival and Samba Show

The Viennese Waltz

The Viennese Waltz is like a fairground ride – the Waltzer of course – a continuously whirling and twirling dance that moves around the floor at a rate of knots. In the early days people use to pass out at the pure exhilaration and excitement of the dance. Even Lord Byron, famous for his debauched and hedonistic lifestyle, condemned it to be 'unchaste', which is saying something… It was banned at the turn of the nineteenth century because it was considered decadent and a bit naughty.

Many of the Ballroom dances have endless amounts of steps to learn, but in the Viennese Waltz there are far fewer and, once you've learned those steps, you are free to go mad. You can really push the boundaries by putting more and more turns in as you go faster and faster around the dance floor. There is not a single straight line in this dance, just turns. So when I do the Viennese Waltz I try to make the turns as grand as I can. I love the great big sweeping movements; they make me think of the Austrian courts in the nineteenth century, with the ladies in their big frocks, with layers of tuille and netting.

Everybody who dances the Viennese Waltz at the beginning gets dizzy, to the point of throwing up. I'm not joking. This is the fastest of all the Ballroom dances, even faster than the Quickstep. I know some people like to get a bit dizzy in that hedonistic way, and you might have been the type of person Lord Byron was describing, and don't get me wrong, I like a bit of excitement, but when I stop I like everything around me to stop at the same time. Leslie Garrett loved the Viennese Waltz, I think it sits with her personality – bright, bubbly and effervescent – which describes the dance perfectly.

Although there aren't that many steps to learn, you have to build up the speed of the dance otherwise you will just go round and round in the centre of the room, getting dizzy and probably crashing into everybody else on the floor. So the motto of this dance is going to be 'gently does it'. Try not to get carried away, and be patient. To get this started we are going to do a little exercise,

which is very very simple. It consists of six steps. That's six steps to the perfect Viennese Waltz, so near and yet, somehow, so far. Now, we are going to do something a little bit different for the ladies here: because this is a rotational dance, we're going to ask the ladies to create a little more poise to the left (i.e. lean your upper body slightly to the left). As you improve your dancing, I would like you to develop this slight poise in all of your ballroom dances, but it particularly helps the rotation of the Viennese Waltz. When we're doing something very rotational the space between the man's and lady's heads will help greatly with the balance of the dance – you'll feel this more when the dance is going at its full speed and you're dashing around the floor, so don't worry if you don't see the relevance at the start but we will build it up as we go. It will become really important to keep this space. I know you've got a lot to think about with your feet and posture and turning, but this little bit of poise will help your dancing enormously.

We're going to assume our normal Ballroom position, with the man standing with perfect posture in front of the lady and the lady, standing with perfect posture, in front of the man, with normal hold. To start, boys face the wall and ladies back the wall, in hold. Then boys step forward with your right foot, ladies step backwards with your left foot. Chaps step to the side with your left foot, ladies step to the side with you right foot. Now close your feet (boys right to left foot, ladies left to right foot). Now, guys, step back with your left foot, ladies step forward with your right foot. Fellas step to the side with your right foot, girls step to the side with left foot. Then close your feet (boys left to right foot, girls left to right foot). That is it. We are ready to start again with the boys, right foot and the girls, left foot. I couldn't have made it

easier if I tried. The easiest thing in the world, it's as simple as falling off a waltzer. So you're basically making a square. I know what you're saying now, there's not a lot of turning going on in this turny dance, 'where's all the turn?' I hear you cry! Well, we're coming to that, don't be so impatient. As we do our box-shaped variation we are going to start to turn it a little bit, to the right. So rather than a box you start to do a circle, so after each 6 steps you'll end up in a different place, to the point where you feel yourself gradually turning round. Keep developing this until you move down the room in a straight line. Now I can hear you saying, 'there are no straight lines in the Viennese waltz!', you've got me, I've been caught out and you're quite right, but the straight line is the movement around the room rather than our actual steps, which are rotational. Did I get a bit technical then? Sorry, I won't do that again, not until the next page anyway. I don't want you to rush into this and think you've cracked it after 10 minutes, so I think you should just make your small box step to start with and develop in from there into a circle. Remember what I said, 'gently does it'.

I asked a teacher one day what the most important thing to remember in the Viennese Waltz was and he replied, 'everything', unfortunately for you, and that's because there's no one single element that's more important than another – they are all cogs in the wheel and principally this is due to the speed of the music. So fellas, I want you to be aware of your perfect posture, the position of your lady (make sure she's on your right front), your wonderful armline, your pure transference of weight, and look left (try not to look at your gorgeous lady in front of you – I know it's hard but try your best). You never seem to get round if you don't have a good posture, I'm warning you.

Viennese Waltz

The music is 3/4 time like the English Waltz, but double the speed. So that's about 60 bars per minute. Johann Strauss was a very famous Waltz composer, so many of his tunes work, like the *Blue Danube* and *Tales from the Vienna Woods*. The Viennese Waltz has a special rhythm. It's still a three-count, but the second beat is rushed a little, leaving a short breathing space between the second and third beats. A truly authentic performance of a Strauss Waltz will rush the second beat in this manner, imparting a special lilt to the music and to the dance. For a more modern tune go for *Iris* by the Goo Goo Dolls, which is one of my favourites, or Alicia Keyes's *If I ain't got you*.

I feel I've been a little bit firm with you today but once you've mastered this dance it will make you feel fabulous as you whizz around the floor.

Viennese Opera Ball

Natural turn

The Natural Turn commences facing diagonally to the centre and ends facing diagonally to the centre.

STEP 1
Man Step forward right foot, turning right
Lady Step backwards left foot, turning right

STEP 2
Man Step to the side left foot, still turning
Lady Step to the side right foot, still turning

STEP 3
Man Close right foot to left foot
Lady Close left foot to right foot

Ideas for a basic dance sequence

Natural Turn – as many as you want, with right foot Change Step into Reverse Turn, with left foot Change Step, into Natural Turn

STEP 4
Man Step backwards left foot, turning right

STEP 5
Man Step to the side right foot, still turning

STEP 6
Man Close left foot to right foot

Lady Step forward right foot, turning right

Lady Step to the side left foot, still turning

Lady Close right foot to left foot

Reverse turn

The Reverse Turn commences facing diagonally
to the wall and ends facing diagonally to the wall.

STEP 1
Man Step forward left foot,
turning left

STEP 2
Man Step to the side and
slightly backwards right foot,
still turning

STEP 3
Man Cross left foot in front of
right foot

Lady Step backwards right foot,
turning left

Lady Step to the side left foot,
still turning

Lady Close right foot to left foot

STEP 4
Man Step backwards right foot, turning left

STEP 5
Man Step to the side left foot, still turning

STEP 6
Man Close right foot to left foot

Lady Step forward left foot, turning left

Lady Step to the side and slightly backwards right foot, still turning

Lady Cross left foot in front of right foot

Charge step

The Charge Step links the Natural Turn to the Reverse Turn and vice versa

STEP 1
Man Step forward right foot

Lady Step backwards left foot

STEP 2
Man Step to the side left foot

STEP 3
Man Close right foot to left foot

Lady Step to the side right foot

Lady Close left foot to right foot

Reverse turn (feet only)

The Reverse Turn feet only demonstrates the crossing position on step 3 for the man and step 6 for the lady.

STEP 1
Man Step forward left foot, turning left
Lady Step backwards right foot, turning left

STEP 2
Man Step to the side and slightly backwards right foot, still turning
Lady Step to the side left foot, still turning

STEP 3
Man Cross left foot in front of right foot
Lady Close right foot to left foot

STEP 4
Man Step backwards right foot, turning left
Lady Step forward left foot, turning left

STEP 5
Man Step to the side left foot, still turning
Lady Step to the side right foot, still turning

STEP 6
Man Close right foot to left foot
Lady Cross left foot in front of right foot

History

There are many theories on the origins of the Viennese Waltz and where and when it dates back to, but it is definitely the oldest of the Ballroom dances. Some say it was danced in the twelfth/thirteenth centuries and was called the Nachtanz from Bavaria. The French claim it, by the end of the sixteenth century, not as a Waltz but as a Volta danced to folk music – presumably in a 3/4 rhythm. The Italians, not to be left out, claim the word volta, meaning 'the turn'. And the Norweigans too. There is even a painting of Queen Elizabeth I of England dancing the Volta with the Earl of Leicester, to be found as Penshurst Place in Kent today.

A much closer relative of the Viennese Waltz, however, would be the Ländler which was danced in Austria in the eighteenth century. Peasants danced the Ländler and the nobility disapproved because of its 'lasciviousness' (the ladies' ankles were visible – simply shocking!) You can see a Ländler being danced in *The Sound of Music* funnily enough; it's about the only time I've seen a Ländler, not being an Austrian folk dancer myself (but not knocking it until I've tried it of course!). But the quickest way to popularise something is to ban it; it was even said there was 'proof that Waltzing is the main weakness of the body and mind of our generation'. The Congress of Vienna (the dance was credited to help put the ambassadors in a good frame of mind to settle the mess after Napoleon's first retirement) the compositions by Vienna's famous Waltz lovers, Josef Lanner, Josef and Johann Strauss made the Viennese Waltz ever more popular. Fabulous dance halls such as the Zum Sperl and the Apollo opened. In 1816 the English took hold of the Waltz, however in 1833 Miss Celbart, in her book on appropriate behaviour and etiquette called it 'a dance of too loose character for maidens to perform'. Lord Byron too had his say in his poem, *The Waltz*. The dance has always had political associations and was even called the 'Marseillaise of the heart' by one Viennese critic, Eduard Hanslick.

Things have changed a bit since then and it is now considered a beautiful classical Ballroom dance. Paul Krebs was a hugely successful German dance teacher from Nurenberg who, in the 1950s, was famed for his dancing in Blackpool in competitions, combining the traditional Waltz with steps of the English style of Viennese Waltzing and in 1963 it was added to the International Standard Ballroom Dances. From the 1960s until the 1980s much discussion took place between the English and German powers that be over standardising which steps were allowed in competition routines; mercifully at some stage they agreed – now we just get on and dance it!

Demonstration of the Waltz

Waltzers and Waltzing

The Mall
Kensington

My dear Gerty

You say that as you know I go out a good deal you would like me to give you my opinion on this subject of "Waltzers & Waltzing"

"Well!— I have "danced" with a short man who held me out at arm's length and walked with me

"With a tall man who squeezed me up against his waistcoat and ambled with me

With a big man who walked over me

With a little one who walked under me.

With a conversational one who trotted about laughing at his own weak witticisms

With a dignified one who strolled about with me in forbidding silence

With an energetic one who strode about knocking me against the other dancers.

With an even more energetic one who pranced all round me treading on my toes

But Jack's the only man who ever "waltzed" with me

The Jive

The Jive is the newest of all the dances to become one of the standardised Latin American dances. Because this dance came out of the social climate of the Second World War, when the guys and girls didn't know when they would next get to dance together, it was celebrated as a fabulous new frenzied style of dancing, where almost anything went. It became a huge release and escape and you were taken away to another place and time. That's what's great about it. I love the fact that a dance can transport you to another world. It's amazing to think a dance can take you away from the horrors in your life and for a few short moments your spirit can be lifted and re-energised. That's what dancing in general is all about for me. Obviously I wasn't around at that time but I do know that dancing can re-invigorate the soul. It's an excuse to let your hair down and I'm glad that it was a dance that enabled them to do exactly that. All dances have this capacity and they can be seen as a reflection of the social climate of their time. For some reason the Jive seems to have a bigger impact, I suppose because it's the newest and most poignant; it affected the whole world. Like all dances it develops and evolves, and so it isn't the same as the one danced at that time, but it still has that sense of escapism.

I love dances that have a bit of a story or a reason for dancing them. Whether I choreograph a story into them or there is a story that underpins the dance, this is what motivates me. In the Jive, I try to use the choreography to show that freedom of expression, the sense of throwing your legs about and letting go, which is so inherent in the dance. It has many elements – lindy hop, rock'n'roll, swing, jitterbug – which makes it a lively high tempo dance, with the feeling of 'anything goes', but you have to maintain a level of technique otherwise it gets messy… and a bit dangerous. We don't have any of the high lifts of the pure rock'n'roll dances in Jive – it's actually an illegal manoeuvre – as Len would say, 'we keep it strictly on the floor'.

We're going to start gently on this one, which we have done with all of the high tempo dances, as I think it's probably the wise way to go. We don't want a groin strain or a hamstring injury before you even get going. I've got two little exercises that are almost the same thing, one very gentle and the other a little more upbeat. So we're going to start off with the slower one, to get you into it

because I know what you're like, you boys, you get all excited and rush into it and throw your partner around because you think you know how to do it because you saw Auntie Ethel and Uncle Norman doing it at their Golden Wedding before he put her hip out as he swung her round and she remembered why she'd given up the Jive in the sixties and took up gardening instead. So here we go. Stand in front of your partner facing each other, with a slight gap between you but hold hands (boys, with your right hand take the girl's left hand and take her right hand with your left hand, i.e. a double hand hold). This little exercise is on the spot, so you're not actually moving anywhere, just rocking from side to side. So, boys step to the left with your left foot, girls step to the right with your right foot. Boys then step to the side with your right foot, girls step to the side with your left foot, making sure you change weight (oh, sounds so familiar doesn't it?), so in effect boys you rock left and then right and girls you do the opposite. Then we do a Back Rock – boys steps back on your left foot, girls step back on your right foot and then boys rock forward onto your right foot and girls on your left foot, obviously changing weight.

Now repeat again, side, side, back rock, side, side, back rock. The rhythm is slow, slow, quick-quick. Okay, that's the gentle one. You see, that wasn't too exhausting was it? Now we are going to do the same exercise but slightly quicker and with a little extra. Rather than just rock to the side we are going to do a little Chassé. Now that consists of this: boys start with your left foot, you do a step to the side but don't make it too big because you will just look a twit. So with the boys left foot moving to his left, close your right foot to the left foot and then step to the side again with your left foot. Girls do the natural opposite starting

with you right foot. Then we come back. Boys, starting with your right foot, so that will be side, close, side. Go to the side then close with your left foot and then step to the side again with your right foot. Then boys, with your left foot, and girls with your right foot, do your back rock. The rhythm to this is slow, quick quick, slow, quick quick, quick quick. When I say slow, it's all relative, it isn't that slow, the quick quick should add up to one slow. That's called a Jive Chassé. That's an integral part of the Jive. This has got to be lively, bright and FUN. You don't want to do this on flat feet, you need a bit of bounce in the knees, without going mad obviously.

The point of this exercise is twofold; firstly it's the importance of learning the Back Rock which is crucial to the dance. You could almost stand still for the rest of the dance and, as long as the Back Rock is correct you will remain on the right foot and in the right time. And the second is harmony, because when you develop the dance and the boys twirl the girls under their arms, boys, you will understand the importance of dancing together. If you're in time with each other then the man can lead the lady into another part of the dance with ease and style – because that's what we're looking for – ease and style.

The problems really are keeping in time, not missing the beat and once again we must address the doom that is not transferring weight. How it keeps me up at night, 'woe is me and thrice woe', it's just so lamentable.

The music is 2/4 but you can use 4/4 music – I know it's not right, I can hear you telling me off, but you can use it, it's fine. A classic oldie is Jerry Lewis's *Great Balls of Fire.*

Jive Chassé

The Jive Chassé can be danced to the side,
forward, backwards or turning and is the integral
part of the Jive rhythm.

STEP 1
Man Take a small step to the
side left foot

STEP 2
Man Close right foot to left foot

STEP 3
Man Take a small step to the
side left foot

Lady Take a small step to the
side right foot

Lady Close left foot to right foot

Lady Take a small step to the
side right foot

Ideas for a basic dance sequence

Basic Jive Chassé to the left, then to the right, Back Rock, Change of Place right to left, Back Rock, Change of Place left to right, Back Rock, Change the Hand Behind the Back, Back Rock, Change the Hand again, Change of Place left to right, American Spin

STEP 4
Man Take a small step to the side right foot

STEP 5
Man Close left foot to right foot

STEP 6
Man Take a small step to the side right foot

Lady Take a small step to the side left foot

Lady Close right foot to left foot

Lady Take a small step to the side left foot

Back rock

The Back Rock is normally danced at the beginning and end of every figure

STEP 1
Man Step backwards left foot
Lady Step backwards right foot

STEP 2

Man Replace weight onto right foot

Lady Replace weight onto left foot

Change of place, left to right

1

2

3

The Change of Place can be danced left to right and right to left. Both commence and end with the Back Rock.

STEP 1
Man Take a small step to the side left foot
Lady Take a small step to the side right foot

STEP 2
Man Close right foot to left foot
Lady Close left foot to right foot

STEP 3
Man Take a small step to the side left foot
Lady Take a small step to the side right foot, starting to turn

4

5

STEP 4
Man Step to the side right foot
Lady Step to the side, whilst turning right, left foot

STEP 5
Man Close left foot to right foot
Lady Close right foot to left foot, turning right

STEP 6
Man Facing your partner; take a small side step right foot
Lady Facing your partner; take a side step left foot

STEPS 7 & 8
Man The Back Rock
Lady The Back Rock

6

7

8

Change of place, right to left

STEP 1
Man Step backwards left foot
Lady Step backwards right foot

STEP 2
Man Replace weight onto
right foot
Lady Replace weight onto
left foot

Commence in Open Position with the lady turning to the left. Start and end with a Back Rock.

STEP 3
Man Take a small step to the side left foot
Lady Take a small step to the side right foot, turning left

STEP 4
Man Close right foot to left foot
Lady Close left foot to right foot, still turning

STEP 5
Man Take a small step to the side left foot
Lady Take a small step to the side right foot, turning to face partner

STEP 6
Man Take a small step to the side right foot
Lady Take a small step to the side left foot

STEP 7
Man Close left foot to right foot
Lady Close right foot to left foot

STEP 8
Man Take a small step to the side right foot
Lady Take a small step to the side left foot

5

6

7

8

American spin

The American Spin commences with a Back Rock, the spin for the lady is taken on step 3. Boys, don't forget to catch your partner after you've lead the spin!

STEP 1
Man Take a small step to the side left foot
Lady Take a small step to the side right foot

STEP 2
Man Close right foot to left foot
Lady Close left foot to right foot

STEP 3
Man Take a small step to the side left foot
Lady Step onto right foot and turn right to face partner

1

2

3

STEP 4
Man Take a small step to the side right foot
Lady Take a small step to the side left foot

STEP 5
Man Close left foot to right foot
Lady Close right foot to left foot

STEP 6
Man Take a small step to the side right foot
Lady Take a small step to the side left foot

4

5

6

Change the hand behind the back

STEP 1
Man With left foot, step towards your partner's right side
Lady With right foot, take a small step towards your partner's right side

STEP 2
Man Close right foot to left foot
Lady Close left foot to right foot

STEP 3
Man Step forward left foot, turning right
Lady Step forward right foot

1

2

3

STEP 4

Man Step forward right foot, still turning so as you face your partner
Lady Step to the side left foot to face your partner

STEP 5

Man Close left foot to right foot
Lady Close right foot to left foot

STEP 6

Man Take a small step to the side right foot
Lady Take a small step to the side left foot

Stop and go (1)

The Stop and Go commences in an open hold and can be danced following the Change of Place, Left to Right

STEP 1
Man The back rock
Lady The back rock

STEP 2
Man The back rock
Lady The back rock

STEP 3
Man Step forward left foot
Lady Step forward right foot, turning left

STEP 4
Man Close right foot to left foot
Lady Close left foot to right foot, still turning

Stop and go (2)

STEP 5
Man Step forward left foot
Lady Step backwards right foot

STEP 6
Man Step forward right foot
Lady Step backwards left foot

STEP 7
Man Replace weight onto left foot
Lady Replace weight onto right foot

5

6

7

STEP 8

Man Take a small step to the side right foot
Lady Step forward left foot, turning right

STEP 9

Man Close left foot to right foot
Lady Close right foot to left foot, still turning

STEP 10

Man Take a small step to the side right foot
Lady Step back left foot to face your partner

8

9

10

Whip

The Whip is danced from an open hold and can be danced following the Change of Place, Left to Right or after the Change of Hand Behind the Back.

STEP 1
Man Cross right foot behind left foot

Lady With left foot step towards partner's right side

STEP 2
Man Step to the side left foot

Lady Step forward between your partner's feet right foot

STEP 3
Man Step to the side right foot

STEP 4
Man Close left foot to right foot

STEP 5
Man Step to the side right foot

Lady Step to the side left foot

Lady Close right foot to left foot

Lady Step to the side left foot

Whip (feet only)

Start and finish facing the Line of Direction, follow with the Three Step, Reverse Wave or, if at a corner, Change of Direction. Start and finish with a Back Rock.

STEP 1
Man Cross right foot behind left foot
Lady With left foot step towards partner's right side

STEP 2
Man Step to the side left foot
Lady Step forward between your partner's feet right foot

STEP 3

Man Step to the side right foot
Lady Step to the side left foot

STEP 4

Man Close left foot to right foot
Lady Close right foot to left foot

STEP 5

Man Step to the side right foot
Lady Step to the side left foot

History

Where precisely the Jive originated is not known but it was danced by the negroes all over the South Eastern states of the US and may have been adopted by them from the indigenous Indian population, though some say that its roots were in Africa. Whatever, it was danced competitively by the 1880s, the prize often being a cake, hence the dance also became know as the Cake Walk. Now on the covers of old music scores for Ragtime, including the music of Scott Joplin, you can see couples dancing the Jive and the Cake Walk. Slowly the Jive evolved into the twentieth century, when Ballroom seemed so sedate and faster dances became the rage. Harlem's Savoy Ballroom opened in the 1920s and speedy, jumpy dances called the Swing or the Lindy Hop (named after Lindbergh, first solo trans-Atlantic pilot because dancers spent so much time in the air – as he did and there was even a Triple Lindy), became of the moment. Swing or Jive was born in Harlem. The Jive meant dancing more than ever to the accents in the music, particularly the second and fourth beats in the bar, and was done to blues music. The oldies, progressing round the dance floor in their anti-clockwise fashion, became exasperated by the young ones dancing the non-progressive Jive and attempts were made to ban the Jive from Ballrooms and dance halls. You dance together, boys and girls, or you dance alone; you do not have to stay in contact all the time.

The Euorpeans loved this dance, and it was brought to England by G. I.s during the Second World War, taught to the locals wherever the G. I.s were stationed and it became, danced to 'Swing' music, one of the excitements in the gloom of war. Some said it had a 'corrupting influence' and tried to force it underground.

Today the Jive is still associated with you young ones. It is close to Rock & Roll, Swing and Boogie-Woogie, and is an energetic and energising dance.

Useful websites

www.istd.org
Imperial Society of Teachers of Dancing
Offers dance examinations and can provide you
with a list of dance schools

www.natd.org.uk
National Association of Teachers of Dancing
Offers dance examinations and classes

www.idta.co.uk
International Dance Teachers' Association
Dance teachers and courses all over the world

www.ukadance.co.uk
United Kingdom Alliance of Professional Teachers
of Dancing
Provides help to find your nearest registered dance
teacher

www.dancesport.uk.com
Latest news and information about Ballroom
dancing

www.dancesport-international.com
International dancing news and online shop

www.dtol.ndirect.co.uk
Dance teachers online.

www.antondubeke.com
www.antonanderin.com
Need I say more!

www.supadance.com
Fabulous shoes!

www.ballroomdancing.co.za
Information on Ballroom and Latin American
dancing in South Africa

www.dancedirectory.co.za
All your dance requirements for South Africa

www.dancesportbc.com
Governing body for amateur dancesport in
Cananda

www.cdta.info
Canadian Dance Teachers Association

Picture acknowledgements

Page 3: Fred Astaire and Ginger Rogers in *Flying
Down to Rio*, Bettmann/Corbis
Page 7: GMK/BBC
Page 21: Bettmann/Corbis
Page 41: Bettmann/Corbis
Page 59: BBC/Corbis
Page 78: Pictorial Press
Page 79: Hulton Archive/Getty Images
Page 83: Swim Ink 2, LLC/CORBIS
Page 105: Hulton Archive/Getty Images
Page 108: Topham Picturepoint
Pages 126 and 127: G. Monteleone/CORBIS

Page 131: TopFoto
Page 143: VERZHBINSKY Asya/ArenaPAL/
TopFoto
Page 147: Ronald Grant Archive
Page 165: Hulton-Deutsch Collection/CORBIS
Page 169: Bettmann/Corbis
Page 183: Sipa Press/Rex Features
Page 187: Hulton Archive/Getty Images
Page 197: Hulton-Deutsch Collection/CORBIS
Page 201: Hulton-Deutsch Collection/CORBIS
Page 222: Roger-Viollet/Topfoto
Page 223: Topham Picturepoint